HOW TO WRITE
FOR CHILDREN

HOW TO WRITE FOR CHILDREN

Tessa Krailing

Allison & Busby
Published by W.H. Allen & Co. Plc

An Allison & Busby book
Published in 1988 by
W.H. Allen & Co Plc
44 Hill Street
London W1X 8LB

Printed and bound in Great Britain by
Anchor Brendon Ltd, Tiptree, Essex

ISBN 0 85031 920 X

CONTENTS

ACKNOWLEDGEMENTS

The Author and the Publishers would like to thank the following for the use of copyright material:

Beverley Anderson, The Good Book Guide to Children's Books 1986; The Bodley Head for extracts from *My Darling Villain* by Lynn Reid Banks: copyright © 1977 by Lynn Reid Banks; and from *Babies Need Books* by Dorothy Butler: copyright © Dorothy Butler 1980; Heinemann Educational Books Ltd and Margaret Ramsay Ltd for an extract from *The Thwarting of Baron Bolligrew* by Robert Bolt: copyright © 1966 by Robert Bolt; Pan Books Ltd for an extract from *Substance and Shadow* by Anthea Cohen: copyright © Anthea Cohen 1986; Hamish Hamilton Ltd and The Putnam Young Readers Group for examples taken from *Princess Smartypants* by Babette Cole: copyright © 1986 by Babette Cole; J.M. Dent & Sons Ltd and Lescher & Lescher Ltd for an extract from *The Moonlight Man* by Paula Fox: copyright © Paula Fox 1986; published in the USA by Bradbury Press: Hamish Hamilton Ltd for an extract from *A Long Way From Verona* by Jane Gardam: copyright © 1971 by Jane Gardam; the author for an extract from *Verse and Various* by Charlotte Hough: copyright © Charlotte Hough 1979; Julia MacRae Books and Greenwillow Books (A Division of William Morrow) for extracts from *The Nature of the Beast* by Janni Howker: copyright © 1985 by Janni Howker, first published in Great Britain by Julia MacRae Books in hardback and published in paperback by Fontana Books; Harlequin

Enterprises B.V. for an extract from *The French Summer* by Tessa Kay: copyright © 1984 by Tessa Kay: All rights reserved. Reproduction by permission of the publisher, Harlequin Enterprises B.V., Fribourg Branch, 6 Route de Beaumont, CH 1700 Fribourg, Switzerland; Hamish Hamilton Ltd and Lescher & Lescher Ltd for an extract from *Journey by First Class Camel* by E.L. Konigsburg: copyright © 1982 by E.L. Konigsburg. Originally published in the USA as *Journey to an 800 Number*. Published in Great Britain 1983 under the title *Journey by First Class Camel*; the author and Victor Gollancz Ltd for an extract from *Dinky Hocker Shoots Smack* by M.E. Kerr: copyright © 1972 by M.E. Kerr. Reprinted by permission of Harper & Row, Publishers, Inc: BBC Books for an extract from *Writing for the BBC*, compiled and edited by Norman Longmate; Penguin Books Ltd for an extract from *Divide and Rule* by Jan Mark (Kestrel Books, 1979), copyright © 1979 by Jan Mark, reprinted by permission of Harper & Row, Publishers, Inc.; Penguin Books Ltd and Greenwillow Books (A Division of William Morrow) for extracts from *The Way to Sattin Shore* by Philippa Pearce (Kestrel Books, 1983), copyright © 1983 by Philippa Ann Pearce; the author for an extract from *Unleaving* by Jill Paton Walsh: copyright © 1976 by Jill Paton Walsh. Reprinted by permission of Farrar, Straus and Giroux, Inc.; Faber & Faber Ltd for an extract from *Conversations with Ayckbourn* by Ian Watson: copyright © 1981 by Ian Watson; Samuel French Ltd for an extract from *The Plotters of Cabbage Patch Corner* by David Wood: copyright © 1972 by David Wood; *Books for Your Children* for an extract from an article by Diana Wynne Jones, pub. 1981.

The author would also like to thank Gwynneth Ashby, Dianne and Stanley Doubtfire, John Escott, Cathy Howes, Shirley Hughes, Geoffrey Lamb, Brenda Little, Fiona Reynoldson, Brenda Stones, and Ann Thwaite for their help, advice, and encouragement.

1

WHY WRITE FOR CHILDREN?

Why write for children?

Well, there's really only one possible motive for any kind of writing: namely, that there's a book inside you demanding to be written and you won't be happy until it's safely down on paper. It doesn't matter whether that book is a learned philosophical treatise or a picture story for five-year-olds, the compulsion is the same.

Is that the case with you?

Perhaps at this stage "compulsion" may seem too strong a word. Perhaps you have an idea for a story that you want to write for children, but you are not sure how to tackle it. What you are looking for is guidance, some practical advice that will help you crystallise your idea into an entertaining, well-crafted, and – with luck – saleable children's book. So here goes.

Let's start by exploding a few myths.

First, that children's books are easier to write than adult novels. Not true, I'm afraid. Admittedly the structure and the language you use may be simpler than for an adult novel, but simplicity is not always easy to achieve. As in most myths, there's an element of truth in that the books may be shorter – although not necessarily so. However, the quality of writing required is certainly no lower than for an adult novel and may in some respects be higher. It is not a lesser art, merely a different one.

Myth number two: that it is easier to get a children's book

published than an adult novel. Again, there's a tiny grain of truth here: these days the adult fiction market is becoming so rigidly structured that it is increasingly difficult to break into it with a slightly offbeat idea. The children's book market is more flexible. There is still room for the writer whose book doesn't quite fit into any particular genre. All publishers, though, are notoriously reluctant to take risks, so you'll have to convince at least one of them that you have something new and interesting to offer which is worth a little risk-taking.

Myth number three: that it is a good idea to start your literary career by writing for children and work your way up. Fatal. If it's an adult novel you're burning to write, then go ahead and do it. You'll never write a good children's book unless you put your heart and soul into it, so it's no use keeping the best of yourself in reserve for something you intend doing later on.

Myth number four: that most children's writers are failed adult novelists anyway. Then how about Penelope Lively, Nina Bawden, Jane Gardam, Roald Dahl, Peter Dickinson, Joan Aiken, to name but a few? Become a children's writer and you will find yourself in excellent company.

Now, having dispelled some of the myths, let's take a look at the more positive reasons why you should want to write for children.

An indelible impression

At a recent get-together of two Writer's Groups people were asked to bring along a short reading from their favourite book. No fewer than three of them chose *The Wind in the Willows*. E. Nesbit's *The Enchanted Castle* was Noel Coward's lifelong favourite, according to his biographer, Cole Lesley. It was found open on his bedside table the night he died. The fact is that books we read and loved when we were young leave an indelible impression on us. In some curious and subtle way they've entered our subconscious.

Here is the opening of *The Wind in the Willows*:

The Mole had been working very hard all the morning, spring-cleaning his little home. First with brooms, then with dusters; then on ladders and steps and chairs, with a brush and a pail of whitewash; till he had dust in his throat and eyes, and splashes of whitewash all over his black fur, and an aching back and weary arms. Spring was moving in the air above and in the earth below and around him, penetrating even his dark and lowly little house with its spirit of divine discontent and longing. It was small wonder, then, that he suddenly flung down his brush on the floor, said "Bother!" and "O blow!" and also "Hang spring-cleaning!" and bolted out of the house without even waiting to put on his coat.

I have only to read those words to feel a tingling sense of anticipation. Something's coming and it's going to be good. I know it's good because it's familiar. It's reliable. I can depend upon this book to transport me into another world where I shall be entertained and entranced and sometimes a little scared. Above all, I shall be with friends I've known for a very long time, friends I can trust.

I don't feel a bit like that about the adult novel I read last week, good though it was. These days I'm not so impressionable. Too many other factors have entered my life, clouding that intensity of vision I had as a child and making it more difficult for me to enter other worlds. The only way I can recapture those sensations is by taking my old friends down from the bookshelf and blowing the dust off their jackets.

Why is it that children have this amazing ability to lose themselves totally in the world of the imagination?

Mainly, I think, it is because their minds are so fresh and receptive. There hasn't yet been time for them to get clogged up with the many drives and anxieties of adult life. Still free spirits, they can move easily between fantasy and reality without being in any danger of confusing the two worlds. But whichever world they inhabit, they are constantly absorbing new ideas and information. Everything they see, hear, read, or watch on television is making that indelible mark that will probably last, if only subconsciously, for the rest of their lives.

Which means that the book you are about to write may well play a significant part in the formation of someone's character.

What a responsibility!

Perhaps it is best not to think about that too much: it could be inhibiting. The point I'm trying to make is that children's books *matter*. They are important. Second-best just won't do in this field, as indeed in any other when it comes to writing. You have to go for gold.

The child inside

Do you have a clear mental picture of the child for whom you are writing your story? Perhaps it is your own son or daughter. Or your grandchild. Or one of the children you teach, if you happen to be a teacher.

Forget them all.

I wrote my first children's book while I was still teaching. My class of nine-year-olds were mad about dinosaurs and always clamouring for stories about them, so rather rashly I said I would write one. Driving home from school I hatched up an idea about a lady dinosaur called Minerva, who was alive and well and had been living for the past few million years under the Mendip Hills. Only now she had developed toothache...

Well, it was a starting point. The strange thing was that as soon as I began to write I lost sight of the children in my class altogether. I was writing this for *me*! And it was with this realisation that the story really caught fire.

The trouble is that if you try writing objectively, for some child or children "out there", it is all to easy to fall into the trap of writing *down* to your readers. Try as hard as you may, a note of condescension creeps in, bringing with it a sense of distance between you and them. Next thing you know, you are toppling over the edge into that awful tweeness or cosiness which typifies the worst kind of children's writing. And of course, children can spot insincerity a mile off. They are not fooled for an instant.

So the child you should really be writing for is the child inside yourself, that part of you still capable of wonder and enthusiasm and imaginative leaps into fantasy. It's important, of course, not to confuse being child*like* with being child*ish*. It's that freshness of vision you're after, the ability to see things as if for the first time instead of through a fog of world-weary adult cynicism. Difficult? Not necessarily.

That same class of nine-year-olds had listened enthralled to C.S. Lewis's *The Lion, the Witch and the Wardrobe*, which I read to them during the autumn term. At Christmas we worked together on a huge picture covering one wall of the classroom, depicting the moment when Santa Claus arrives in Narnia in defiance of the White Witch. We painted the background and stuck on everything bright we could find – cotton-wool snow sprinkled with glitter, foil-covered parcels on the sleigh, and a mass of silver stars in the sky. When it was finished the Headmaster came to see what we'd done. The children and I waited, holding our breath, for his verdict.

"Very nice," he said at last. "Gaudy – but nice."

When he'd gone the children asked me what "gaudy" meant.

"Brilliant," I said. "Brightly-coloured. Beautiful."

They were quite happy with that. But I had just had a profound revelation. Up to that moment I had been looking at that picture through a child's eyes and and it wasn't until an adult came into the room that I was forced to see it in a different light. Yes, it *was* gaudy. Unashamedly, eye-dazzlingly gaudy. But the children and I had thought it was beautiful. It was, I think, at this point that I realised that part of me had never stopped being a child. I make no apologies for the fact. It has stood me in very good stead.

Ah, you may well – and very sensibly – say, but isn't there a danger here? If I write for the child I once was won't my writing be dated? Children have changed. They live in a different world from the world I inhabited when I was young and are subject to totally different influences. How can I be sure that what I write will still be relevant?

Two points. The first is that I never suggested you should write for the child you *once were*. That would be a mistake. It is the child still alive inside you now, the one who's travelled all the way with you since those early years, that you should be aiming at.

Second, emotions don't change. If you can recall on paper your own feelings of fear, happiness, excitement, loneliness, insecurity, and love, then you can climb inside the skin of any modern child or adolescent. The externals don't matter so much – they can be easily researched. It's what goes on inside your characters' hearts and minds that counts.

Dual standards

There is one factor in writing for children that doesn't occur in other kinds of fiction, and that's the necessity to please not only the readership you are aiming at but also the adults who stand between you and that readership. By this I mean publishers and booksellers as well as the parents, grandparents, aunts, uncles, teachers, etc who you hope will buy your books. Unless *they* like your work it may never reach the audience it's intended for.

Is this need to operate on two levels at once a real problem?

I don't believe it is. It seems to me that if a book is "true", in the sense that it genuinely represents the best you can do and isn't merely a contrivance to get yourself into print, then its appeal will be universal. Many highly successful books have attracted a far wider range of readers than their authors could at first have imagined. Look at *Watership Down*. Or *The Lord of the Rings*. Or *The Secret Diary of Adrian Mole aged 13¾*. The practice of labelling books as suitable for specific age groups is largely a marketing device, since a bright eight-year-old can easily cope with a book intended for an older child. Conversely, a 14-year-old may still derive enormous pleasure from re-reading a book he first enjoyed when he was nine.

Come to that, so may a 40-year-old.

As for publishers, they are perfectly capable of spotting "a good read' when they see one, no matter what age group it is aimed at. In any case none of these considerations should enter your head when you start writing. My experience is that a book will find its own level, so it simply isn't worth worrying about. *To thine own (writing) self be true*, and let instinct be your guide.

Are you sitting comfortably?

Then we're almost ready to begin. I just have one suggestion to make, that you should visit the children's section of your local library and take a look at what's on offer.

You may find it quite an eye-opener.

There is no need to attempt an in-depth survey of the entire range of children's literature. Just borrow a few books you like the look of and read them purely for pleasure. However, if you feel in need of guidance, a recommended reading list can be found at the back of this book. It gives details of the books specifically quoted or mentioned in the text, but if you make a note of the authors you'll probably find that any of their titles will make interesting reading.

Be careful, though. Even if you find an author you admire tremendously, don't allow him/her to influence you too much.

The last thing you want to do is try to imitate other writers, since your best hope of success lies in being different from everyone else. Developing your own unique style, seeing things with a fresh eye – that is what writing is all about.

So now let's get started. And remember, second best won't do. We're going for gold.

2

GETTING STARTED

By far the greatest part of this book will be concerned with the writing of fiction. In my view this is only right and proper. As Ann Thwaite – herself an author of both fiction and non-fiction – says: "Books about castles or transport or the weather are useful, of course, but they can only teach the child about castles or transport or the weather – whereas good fiction, good stories, can tell a child about human relationships and the possibilities of life itself and other things far more important than castles, transport and the weather."

The next four chapters, therefore, will deal with the craft of fiction-writing in general, since whichever type of book you decide to write – or for whichever age group – there is so much that can be universally applied.

The first spark

A writer is often asked, "Where do you get your ideas from?" Well, of course, ideas come in many ways and may be sparked off by something concrete, such as an incident observed in the street, or by something far more difficult to define, a slowly evolving process of thought. Once I even dreamed about a character, who came complete with her name – Dame Barbara Blanchflower, famous female inventor, in her royal blue tracksuit – and that dream was so vivid that eventually a whole book grew up around her *(Washington and the Marrow Raiders)*. Usually, though, I find the first idea is not enough: it needs another to fuse with it before you get spontaneous combustion. In Dame Barbara's case it wasn't until I put her together with Washington – a robot who looked exactly like a real boy and who was, naturally enough, Dame Barbara's invention – that a story was born.

What should you do when an idea first comes? Well, if you're an organised person you probably reach for your notebook and write it down quickly before you forget it. On the other hand, you may prefer to leave it alone for a while and let it take its chance. My own feeling is that if an idea is strong and significant enough to form the basis of a book, then it is in no danger of allowing itself to be forgotten. It will keep coming back again and again, battering itself against the door of your consciousness and demanding to be written. However, the way you choose to work will largely be dictated by the sort of person you are, so if you feel happier keeping an "ideas" book, then that's what you should do.

Getting to know your characters

Most writers would agree, I think, that an idea needs a period of gestation. It is during this "growing" stage that you can look at it from all angles, size up its potential and decide how best to put it to work. At a guess, your idea will come in the form of a character or characters in a certain situation; or you may think of the situation first and put some characters into it. Either way, those characters are going to be the most important factor in your story. The situation is needed to provide the initial conflict – and conflict, of course, is the stuff of which fiction is made – but it is the characters who must carry the story from that point onwards, and it is they who must engage your reader's interest. That's why, at this stage, it is worth spending a little time and trouble on getting to know them.

Again, how you do this depends entirely on your own preferences. It can be a purely mental exercise, in which you spend every available moment thinking about those characters until they begin to come alive – and sometimes they spring to life so vividly that they seem almost more real than the friends and family with whom you come into daily contact.

Another way is to write down as many details about them as you can, such as date of birth, colour of hair, colour of eyes, favourite food, favourite TV programmes, etc. This background material gives them substance, and will also help you to avoid making obvious mistakes, such as changing the colour of their eyes halfway through the story. One word of warning, though: don't get them so rigidly fixed in your mind that they have no room to breathe. Allowing characters to grow and change is what gives a book its dynamism. Sometimes they may even take you, the author, by surprise and when that happens you know that somehow, miraculously, they've acquired a life of their own. Now your problem is to keep them under control!

Pre-planning

How much pre-planning should you do?

Again, this is entirely up to you. You may find it helpful to write down a list of chapter numbers or headings on one side of a sheet of paper and set against them a rough idea of what is going to happen in each one. Some writers go further than this, working out time charts and planning in detail the contents of each chapter before they are ready to start. Clearly this is a matter of temperament. Most writers, when they begin, have at least a vague idea where they are going, but may not be too sure of the exact route that will take them there. They prefer to leave themselves free to alter course if something interesting crops up to take them off in a new direction. This makes the writing of a book an exciting, even dangerous, voyage of discovery.

However, if you are lucky enough to be commissioned to write a book, the publisher will need a synopsis before he can offer a contract. He may also ask to see the first chapter. Now this first chapter is all-important. It sets the scene, establishes the characters, and provides the impetus to get the story under way. My own experience is that if I write the synopsis first it may well kill the whole story stone dead; but once Chapter One is written everything becomes much easier. I have "caught" the characters on paper and the book has already taken off. Now I can write the synopsis because I have a much better idea of how the story is likely to turn out. It doesn't matter if subsequently I find I want to deviate slightly from my original synopsis: no publisher will object to changes that result in a better finished product.

So let's take a look at that all-important first chapter.

Where should the story begin?

This is not such a foolish question as it sounds. The most common fault among novice writers is to begin a book too far back, or alternatively to plunge their readers headlong into confusion by failing to set the scene adequately first. And remember, when you are writing for children clarity is vital, especially at the beginning. If a child is confused he is far less likely to persist with a story than an adult. So you must catch his interest as quickly as possible, and hold it by involving him in a situation he finds intriguing.

A marvellous piece of advice about the right place to start was given to me by Dianne Doubtfire, whose book *The Craft of Novel-Writing* is a companion volume in this series. "A good place to begin a story," she said, "is just before a change takes place in the life of your central character."

How many books have you read which open with a journey to a new location? Or the arrival of a visitor to shatter hitherto peaceful lives? Or a sudden alteration in family fortunes, usually for the worse? All these openings involve some sort of change which will pitchfork the central character into a situation of conflict.

When George, in C. Day Lewis's book *The Otterbury Incident*, is wondering where to begin, his English teacher tells him to "jump right into the deep end of the story, don't hang about on the edge". In other words, it's a good idea to open with a big scene, something dramatic that will grab your reader's attention and hold it long enough for you to get the characters established.

Alternatively, you can establish a character so strongly that the reader is hooked anyway. Take this opening from Jane Gardam's *A Long Way from Verona*:

> I ought to tell you at the beginning that I am not quite normal having had a violent experience at the age of nine. I will make that clear at once because I have noticed that if things seep out slowly through a book the reader is apt to feel let down or tricked in some way when he eventually gets the point.
>
> I am not, I am glad to say, mad, and there is so far as I know no hereditary madness in my family. The thing that sets me apart from other girls of my age – which is to say thirteen – is that when I was nine a man came to our school – it was a private kindergarten sort of school where you could go from five upwards but most girls left when they were eleven unless they were really stupendously dumb – to talk to us about becoming writers.

In that passage the character of Jessica Vye comes over so vividly that she immediately engages our sympathy. So she regards herself as being "not quite normal"? Well, we're all familiar with that feeling: who hasn't at some time or other felt

21

that they were out of step with the rest of the human race? We can identify with Jessica. That means we want to know what happens to her.

Whose viewpoint?

This question of reader identification is particularly significant when it comes to writing for children, because of their ability to lose themselves so completely in a story that they become totally involved with the central character. For the period of time during which they are reading or listening to a story they *are* that character, and for this reason it's important to avoid any sudden lapses or changes of viewpoint which will break their concentration.

It may be helpful to consider the options when it comes to deciding through whose eyes you are going to tell the story. You have, broadly speaking, three choices:

1 *Omniscient viewpoint*
This is sometimes known as "author talking" or a "God's eye" viewpoint. In other words, the story is being told in a detached, impersonal manner and not as experienced by any one character. It is a perfectly valid style of storytelling, very popular in 19th century fiction, but not really to be recommended when writing for children.

At this point I have to come clean and confess that, in my ignorance, I began my first children's book, *A Dinosaur Called Minerva*, with just such a piece of omniscient scene-setting.

From the depths of the cave called Dragon's Tooth there came a roar so mighty that the ground shook, sending clumps of sandy soil tumbling down the steep sides of Silverton Combe. Drivers leaned out of their cars, peering up into the sky to see if a jet had just broken the sound barrier, rabbits emerged from their burrows with the speed of champagne corks and startled birds left their trees for the safety of the sky.

In the village of Silverton, just below the caves, cups and saucers trembled on their shelves and the landlord of the "George and Dragon" apologised to his wife for his indigestion, which had been troubling him, he said, since lunchtime. It was then six o'clock.

It was over in a few seconds. Some earth movement, suggested the experts, deep in the network of limestone caves beneath Mendip. Most likely the crumbling walls of an underground tunnel had at last collapsed.

Local people shook their heads wisely and said no, it was more likely to have been the dragon again.

Simon Peter Richard Ogden, known to his friends as Sprog, was not in the best of spirits. He stood leaning against a post outside Bath station, thoughtfully kicking a wire litter-bin.

Fortunately, from that point onwards, events were related as seen through Sprog's eyes. If I had continued any longer in the omniscient viewpoint I would probably have lost my readers. As it was, I think it worked – just. But if I were to write that book again, now, I would almost certainly begin it differently.

2   Third person viewpoint

This is by far the most commonly used form of narrative. It enables you, while maintaining your role as storyteller, to get inside the skin of one – or possibly more – of your characters, so that the reader can share the thoughts and feelings of that character and thus feel directly involved. I say "possibly more", but when writing for children it's advisable to limit your viewpoint characters to two or three at the most. In fact, unless it's absolutely necessary – ie you have two equally important characters and need to tell the story through both pairs of eyes – it's safer to limit yourself to one viewpoint. This way you are far more likely to hold your reader's interest throughout. Certainly younger children find it very difficult to take an imaginative leap out of one character, with whom they have already begun to identify, into another.

By far the most confusing thing you can do is to change viewpoints within the same scene. This causes that sudden jolt and break of concentration that I mentioned earlier. Here is an example:

> Sarah snatched the book out of Pete's hands and held it to her chest. "You're not to look at it," she said fiercely. "It's private."
> Pete wondered what she was making all the fuss about. Just a load of old poems, that's all it was, written in Sarah's round, childish hand. Nothing significant.
> Sarah turned away to hide her hot, embarrassed face.

To be suddenly thrust into Pete's mind, even for one brief paragraph, not only undermines the reader's sense of identification with Sarah, but strikes a false note. In real life we never know what the other person is thinking and that's why human relationships can be so difficult and so full of mystery. Rewritten from Sarah's viewpoint only, that scene would read like this:

> Sarah snatched the book out of Pete's hands and held it to her chest. "You're not to look at it," she said fiercely. "It's private."
> Pete stared at her in amazement. She could see he was wondering why on earth she was making such a fuss about a poetry book and turned away to hide her hot, embarrassed face.

3 *First person viewpoint*

Stories told in the first person have many advantages but also some disadvantages. The main advantage is a high level of reader involvement: everything that happens is seen through one character's eyes and you know exactly what's going on inside his head. You are, of course, limited strictly to that one viewpoint; however, this limitation can be converted into a strength, as we've seen.

Perhaps the main difficulty to overcome is the awkwardness with which your viewpoint character must speak of himself. For example, he can't really say anything too complimentary or he may come across as big-headed. You also have to guard against too much introspection.

So how do you decide whether to tell your story in the first person or the third?

Usually your decision is dictated by the type of story you want to write, but if you have any doubts it may be a good idea to try it out both ways. To give you an example, I was experimenting recently with the opening of a story for young adults. It concerns a girl who wants to leave school early, against the advice of her teachers and friends, so that she can stay at home and housekeep for her beloved but somewhat disorganised father – a highly unfashionable ambition. My first attempt went something like this:

> Pippa climbed the hill behind Monkswood and stood with her back against a beech tree, gazing down at the house she loved. She knew every stick and stone of it. It was her home. And tomorrow she would be leaving school for good . . .

Boring, isn't it? Just like every other book you've ever read – and there must be dozens – which start with the heroine on top of a hill, gazing fondly down at the dear old homestead.

So I tried putting it into the first person. Taking me by surprise, it came out like this:

> On the day I left school for good I thought that all my worries were over. How wrong can you be?

Obviously this is the opening of a completely different book. No more sentimental mooning about on hilltops. This heroine will be far more down to earth. I had found my "voice".

Getting the voice right

This business of finding the right "voice" is possibly the single most vital key to getting your story off to a good start. It sets the tone for the rest of the book and gives it that stamp of individuality which makes it different from any other. No matter whether you're writing in the first or third person, your opening paragraph will point the way.

Take these two contrasting openings:

The sound of a flute awakened Catherine Ames. She went from her bed and knelt on the window seat's worn cushion. Her face close to the rusted screen, she listened intently, wondering who it was who walked, playing music, along the narrow street below. But as the music grew fainter, the question that plagued her days rose in her mind. It was like a pain from which only an odd event – a flute played in the middle of the night – could distract her.

Where was he? Where was her father?

The Moonlight Man by Paula Fox

When my mother married Mr F. Hugo Malatesta the First, she sent me to stay with my father while she went on a honeymoon. To my mother he was always your father, the camel-keeper. My mother divorced him because of his camel.

Journey by First Class Camel by E.L. Konigsburg

Two very different voices. The first, using the third person, tells us clearly that this is going to be a thoughtful, sensitive book, full of atmosphere. The second, using the first person, prepares us for a witty, punchy read about some off-beat characters. Now we know what to expect and can settle down in the appropriate frame of mind. We may enjoy both books equally, but they will demand from us, as readers, different responses. This underlines the need to be consistent. Once you have started your book using a certain voice then you must stick to it. It would be unforgivable to open in a bright and breezy fashion and then switch to stark melodrama halfway through: your readers would feel they'd been let down.

This question of "voice" is of course bound up with style, but they're not quite the same thing. Your style is you, and –

provided you are writing naturally and not trying to copy other people – will colour everything you do. It's far more subtle and deep-rooted than the "voice" which can, and should, be different for each book. An actor may be convincing in many different roles, but to each he brings that special quality which is his own unique style.

Setting the scene

Setting the scene is not merely a question of describing the geographical location where your story is to take place, but embraces the whole tricky business of conveying to the reader, as unobtrusively as possible, a wealth of information about the imaginary world he is about to enter. The keyword here is "unobtrusively". Nothing is more offputting to the reader than to be faced with three or four pages of facts about the central character's past life before the story properly begins. Yet those facts may be vital to his understanding. So how do you get them over?

Let's look at how a master practitioner sets about the task.

Here is Kate Tranter coming home from school in the January dusk – the first to come, because she is the youngest of her family. Past the churchyard. Past the shops. Along the fronts of the tall, narrow terrace houses she goes. Not this one, nor this one, nor this . . .

Stop at the house with no lit window.

This is home.

Up three steps to the front door, and feel for the key on the string in her pocket. Unlock, and then in. Stand just inside the door with the door now closed, at her back.

Stand so, in the hall. Ahead, to the right, the stairs. Ahead, to the left, the passage to the kitchen; in the wider part, by the back door, a round, red, friendly eye has seen her – the reflector of her bicycle.

To the left of the hall, Granny's room.

Kate Tranter took a slow breath. She made herself ready to start across the floor to the stairs – to cross the dark beam that came from her grandmother's room through the gap where her grandmother's door stood open.

The Way to Sattin Shore by Philippa Pearce

We now know a great deal about Kate Tranter. We know she's the youngest in her family and the kind of house she lives in. We also know the geography of that house – and it's important we should be familiar with it because of the story which follows. If it weren't important the author wouldn't have put it in. And it's all being conveyed through action. There's something going on, a picture for us to watch that's telling us far more than any leaden lump of description.

We've also discovered that Kate is afraid of her grandmother. It's not stated in so many words, but the implication is there. Her real problem, of course, is a great deal more complex, but we shall learn about it gradually, as the story unfolds. There's no need to rush things at this stage; it's enough for us to know that all is not well.

But surely, you may say, it's not essential for the central character to have a problem, not in a children's book? Well, unless your characters *want* something, and unless they have to overcome some kind of obstacle that stands between them and the object of their desire, you don't really have a story. That is, of course, a piece of gross oversimplification: nonetheless, a story in which the central character sails through situations with no difficulties at all will inevitably lack both depth and interest.

Another way of conveying information without being too heavy-handed is through dialogue, especially between two people who are meeting each other for the first time. In a few short sentences you can tell your reader a great deal about who your characters are and how they came to be in this situation, certainly as much as he needs to know at that stage. The rest can be filtered in later, once you've got the story under way.

Strong colours

When writing for children it is important to weave some strong colours into that first chapter, so that they have something to grab hold of which will lead them forward into the next. Janni Howker's remarkable book, *The Nature of the Beast*, opens with a collage of newspaper headlines, such as: JOBS BLOW FOR HAVERSTON, THE HAVERSTON BEAST STRIKES AGAIN!, and DOUBLE TRAGEDY FOR LOCAL FARMER. Then she begins:

> Oh, I remember the headlines, but they don't tell the whole story – newspapers never do. They don't know the half of it. Not one half! And even if they did, I reckon they wouldn't care – not about Dad or Chunder, or the trouble I'm in.
> I'll give them headlines! I'll hammer them with headlines until I make this town squint! But I bet you a pound to a pinch of salt that they still won't see the thread. No, they'll not see that all these things are connected up, just like knots in a length of thread...
> And here's me, Bill Coward, Ned Coward's son and Chunder's grandson – nobody. And I'm the only one who really knows about the Beast.

Here are strong colours indeed. Anyone starting to read this book will by now have grabbed the thread and want to carry it through. The forward flowing movement has begun.

Your first chapter is so important that it's worth taking time and trouble over getting it right. Of course you may be lucky and get it right first time. But if your instinct tells you that it could be better, then don't begrudge the extra effort it may cost you. It will be time well spent.

Almost as important as getting the opening of your first chapter right is knowing when to finish it. Don't try to round everything off too neatly; end on a question mark, something that will lead your reader on to the next.

Here's how Janni Howker finished her first chapter:

In the end I got out of bed and went to the window. The rain was still crying down the glass, and Haverston was quiet under a yellowish cloud, with the dark night over the Pennines and the yellow street-lamps below. I stood there, cold, listening to the wind off the night moors. And maybe something else was listening. Something that kills hens and sheep and sometimes men ... Something that hears you, and comes closer ...

No. No. It wasn't like that. That's the thread. I only went to the window to see if my dad was coming home in time to pick up some fish and chips from Danny's. But the chip shop light was out. It was dark. I stood looking into the dark.

3

BRINGING YOUR STORY TO LIFE

When you write a story you are creating a make-believe world in which a set of imaginary characters play their part in a drama that you have invented for them. Yet, if you want to hold your reader's interest, you must convince him that all this is actually happening, that it's as real as the world he inhabits, and that the fate of these characters is important.

So how do you bring your story to life?

Characterisation

The best starting point is undoubtedly the characters themselves, since they form the basis on which you are going to build the whole fabrication. If they are not believable, nothing else will be. You may have noticed, by the way, that I've been careful to use the word "characters" rather than people, since in children's books the central character may well be non-human. But it makes no difference whether your story revolves around a child, an animal, a robot, or a monster from outer space – we must still be able to believe in them.

Finding just the right name can be a great help. Usually it comes with the character, sometimes it takes a little longer, but names seem to have the mysterious, magical power of endowing even inanimate objects with a personality of their own. When I was writing *Washington and the Marrow Raiders* the villain of the piece, Dame Barbara's rival inventor, came into my mind already christened as Dr Lucius Delabole, and at once it seemed inconceivable that he could ever have been called anything else.

How much physical description should you give?

Clearly a complete run-down of height, colouring, age, and body weight as each new character comes on the scene would be boring and unimaginative. Nonetheless you do need to convey some kind of visual image. In my opinion the best way is to pick out one or two unusual features, such as a freckled nose or rimless spectacles, and mention them a couple of times early on to establish that image in the reader's mind. The rest of the detail he can fill in for himself. You can also convey a good deal by their actions. If a man has to stoop as he enters the room, for example, then you needn't state that he's tall.

Actions, too, can tell us what kind of people they are. Rather than stating flatly, "Evadne loved getting others into trouble", it's far better to *show* us Evadne getting someone into trouble. This is where you can also use dialogue to good advantage. Here's Tucker Woolf, in M.E. Kerr's book *Dinky Hocker Shoots Smack!*, talking to his girlfriend Natalia:

> "When I get nervous, I go to the library and hang around. The libraries are filled with people who are nervous. You can blend in with them there. You're bound to see someone more nervous than you are in a library. Sometimes the librarians themselves are more nervous than you are. I'll probably be a librarian for that reason. Then if I'm nervous on the job, it won't show. I'll just stamp books and look up things for people and run back and forth to the staff room sneaking smokes until I get hold of myself. A library is a great place to hide.'

In that speech Tucker has told us far more about himself than could ever have been conveyed in a piece of flat description.

How can you make characters three-dimensional?

If you are writing a realistic story there's no place for the all-good hero or the all-bad villain: they belong to the realm of myth and fairy-tale. Far more interesting is the hero who has a tendency to distort the truth; or the villain who is devoted to his dog. The paradox, the unexpected trait, is what will give your character depth. If you have a child as the central character in your story take care you don't make him a cardboard cut-out to whom things happen while leaving him basically unaffected. But of course, if you're writing from inside the character and not as the detached storyteller, this won't be a danger.

Don't be afraid to make your subsidiary characters slightly – or even outrageously – larger than life. They should be entertaining and memorable, not mere tools of the plot. Often it's these secondary characters that leave the most lasting impression – look at Mr Toad in *Wind in the Willows* – so it's well worth putting a little extra effort into their creation rather than sketching them in with a few perfunctory strokes.

Parents can be a particular hazard. Nina Bawden has this to say about them:

> The books offered to me in my childhood left out the adult world, and even when they didn't, entirely, they never presented adults as children really see them. Not only were they never beastly to children except in a stereotyped, fairy-tale way, but they were never beastly to anyone. They were never the uncertain, awkward, quirky, *dangerous* creatures that I knew adults to be.
>
> *Children's Literature in Education*, No. 14, pub. May 1974

These days writers have a different approach. Paula Fox's *The Moonlight Man*, of which I quoted the opening paragraph in the last chapter, deals with the child of divorced parents who goes to spend her summer vacation with the father she hardly knows. She discovers him to be a liar and a drunkard; nonetheless he challenges her to reassess herself and the values she has been brought up to consider important. Here the characterisation of a parent figure has come a long way from the old bland stereotype.

Even when the story is for younger children, parents can still be portrayed as real, flesh-and-blood human beings, capable of making a wrong decision now and again. To my mind, this has the effect of making them more likeable as well as more interesting. To depict parents, teachers, and adults-in-general as faceless authoritarian cyphers is doing no-one a service, least of all the children you're writing for.

Making a scene of it

Here are two ways of dealing with the same incident:

1 When they reached the wood Mark hung back. "What's the matter?" Susie demanded. "You're not scared, are you?"

"Of course not." He was stung by the scorn in her voice. "It's just that it looks – well, a bit sinister."

"How can it be sinister? It's only a wood, for heaven's sake." Impatiently Susie strode ahead to disappear into the trees.

After a few moments Mark followed, although his heart was beating fast. At once the trees seemed to close in on him, whispering to each other as he passed between them. He could hear Susie moving through the undergrowth and tried hard to catch up, but somehow she eluded him. At last he stood still and when he had caught his breath he called out, "Susie? Sue, where are you?"

There was no answer. Nor could he any longer hear sounds of movement. Everything seemed still and deathly quiet, as if he were completely alone.

2 As soon as they reached the wood Mark hung back. When Susie demanded why, he told her that the wood seemed to him sinister, but she only laughed and strode ahead, disappearing among the trees. After a moment Mark followed, trying hard to catch up; but somehow she eluded him. At last he stood still and called her name, but she didn't answer. He seemed to be completely alone.

The same incident, but I hope you will agree with me that the first version is far more likely to appeal to a young reader than the second. This is because it has been dramatised. Instead of telling the story as a straight piece of narration I've "made a scene of it".

These days we are all – adults as well as children – used to watching a great deal of drama on television, whether in the form of single plays, old films, or soap opera. As a result many writers tend to think quite naturally in terms of "scenes", which means that their stories make a strong impact on young readers already conditioned to expect this kind of treatment. Dramatisation is sometimes called the hidden art of storytelling. As readers, you may be unaware of the reason why a story fails to grab you; you only know that a piece of narrative has been going on for pages and nothing seems to have happened. In fact a lot may have happened, but because it hasn't been dramatised you've missed it.

Remember, though, that each scene must have a purpose, either to further the story or to tell us something significant about the characters. Beautifully written, true-to-life vignettes are fine for soap opera because the stories are open-ended; but a novel must have shape and structure and be heading for a satisfying conclusion.

Dialogue

Children love plenty of conversation in a story. Not only does it help to bring the characters to life, but it also looks interesting on the page, breaking up those wearisome chunks of prose. Again, though, it must be there for a purpose: aimless chit-chat that doesn't lead anywhere will only bore the reader.

The trouble is, of course, that real-life conversations tend to be about ninety per cent chit-chat. But, if you listen hard, you'll realise that amidst all that verbiage about the shocking weather we've been having lately and the chronic state of Aunt Ethel's health are hidden some vital nuggets of information. It's the writer's task to select those nuggets and discard everything that is superfluous. In other words, what may appear on the printed page as natural conversation is in fact nothing of the sort: it is only the writer's skill that creates an illusion of spontaneity.

So how do you make your dialogue appear natural?

It helps if you have an ear for the rhythms and cadences of everyday speech. If you haven't, then you may have to work a little harder, being constantly on your guard against putting stilted, contrived remarks into your character's mouth. A good test is to read aloud what you have written and ask yourself, Does it *sound* right? Better still, put it on to a cassette recorder so that you can listen to it more objectively.

Remember, you can control the pace and mood of a scene by the use of dialogue. Obviously a short, sharp interchange between two characters will convey speed and urgency, whereas a long soliloquy slows the pace right down and suggests a dreamy, introspective mood. On the whole, it is best to keep speeches fairly short when writing for children: if a character does hold forth for any length of time then the subject matter must be so rivetting that there is no danger of your reader's interest being lost.

As far as possible, try to avoid setting your dialogue within the framework of a static situation. Children, being naturally active creatures, tend to talk on the move, so it is far more convincing to have them exchanging remarks while scaling a wall or fishing for tadpoles in a pond. This helps to keep things lively, as well as establishing a strong visual image for the reader to hold in his mind while the dialogue is taking place.

When writing dialogue there are certain accepted conventions which it may be useful to summarize.

1   Always start a new paragraph when you have a change of speaker. If a character makes two consecutive speeches, interrupted by action, they can both be contained within the

same paragraph.

Example:

"Look what I've found." Ralph opened the box to show me a curiously shaped stone studded with tiny fragments of shell. "What do you think it is?"

2   Stylistically it is preferable to use "he said, she said" than to introduce too many variations such as gasped, cried, expostulated, remonstrated, etc. In fact, as readers, we are so used to "he said, she said" that we hardly notice it, however repetitious its use, whereas the introduction of a more unusual verb of speech can be obtrusive. If you do use a variation make sure it justifies its existence by conveying the speaker's manner or tone of voice, rather than being there merely to ring the changes.

3   If you describe a character's actions when he's speaking then you don't need a verb of speech at all. Look again at the example in (1) above. I didn't bother to put "said Ralph" after the first speech because when Ralph went on to open the box it was obvious that it was he who had spoken.

4   If you have only two characters in a scene there is no need to identify them after every speech; the fact that you've started a new paragraph will tell your reader that there has been a change of speaker. You must, of course, establish at the beginning which of them speaks first; and every now and again the reader will need reminding of the speaker's identity, just in case they've lost track. Younger children, especially, could easily be confused by a long sequence of unidentified speech. Ideally we should be able to tell who's who by the way they speak and the things they say, but if the speeches are short that's not always possible.

5   Everyday speech is most commonly characterised by the use of shortened forms, such as we'll, she'd, they've, etc. If used in full they tend to add emphasis, as in "We shall be there, I

promise", or suggests that a character isn't speaking his native tongue. This can of course be turned to advantage if you want to suggest he's speaking rather formal English, with perhaps a slight accent, and is certainly preferable to trying to reproduce his speech phonetically.

6   By the same token, it is best to keep the use of dialect to a minimum. If you have a good ear you can convey regional differences in speech by careful choice of vocabulary, and by the way you structure a sentence. Such devices as phonetic spelling and the use of apostrophes to denote dropped aitches are irritating and, to a child, often incomprehensible. If your story is set in Scotland, for example, it is far better to try to capture the lilt and flavour of the Scottish tongue rather than make your characters express themselves solely in "Scots, wha hae" – type language, which is tedious to read and not particularly convincing.

7   Unspoken thoughts can be set out in a number of ways, but the most commonly used convention is to begin with a capital letter and omit the quotation marks.

Example:
Harry thought, It's a good thing I burned that letter.

It is worth remembering that dialogue will constitute at least a third – possibly more – of your story. Not only does it fulfil the obvious function of furthering the plot, but it can also set the scene, convey a mood, express emotion, or describe action. Above all, it gives your narrative a quality of immediacy. Its importance, therefore, cannot be over-emphasised.

Keeping things moving

When writing for children it is vital to keep the forward thrust of a story going all the time so that the reader feels he's being carried relentlessly onward. If you have ever tried reading aloud to a class of eight-year-olds you will be familiar with that subtle change in the atmosphere, an onset of restlessness, which occurs when a story temporarily loses its way. Perhaps the writer has indulged himself with a few paragraphs of beautifully written but unnecessary description. Or he may have sent his characters off on a brief detour which appears to have nothing to do with the plot. Or maybe he has introduced a character who is just plain boring. Whatever the reason, the tension has been lost – and so has the audience.

Clearly, description *for its own sake* is always a mistake. It is a great temptation, when you're describing a location you know well, to let yourself go with a piece of stunning poetic prose, but the danger is that this will turn out to be a case of "author talking". In other words, you've momentarily stepped outside your viewpoint character to give us an impersonal description of a landscape, which means about as much as a picture postcard sent from abroad. As soon as you step back inside your character then we get an entirely different view, since we're seeing it through his eyes and therefore experiencing his emotional reactions to the scene. Perhaps he finds the landscape beautiful but oppressive; the busyness of a city street may underline his loneliness; or the dark, still waters of the lake suggest menace. In other words, if every piece of description is directly related to the mood and emotions of your viewpoint character, there is no risk of it being superfluous to the plot.

A skilful writer may convey an atmosphere of tension through the most subtle use of description. In Philippa Pearce's *The Way to Sattin Shore*, Kate Tranter goes for the first time to the place which is the centre of a family mystery, where someone – perhaps her own father – was drowned ten years ago.

39

She looked right across the estuary to the other side. She could see, in the furthest distance, houses here and there among trees. No people; but perhaps the distance was too great for her to distinguish people. There were no people visible anywhere, on that side or this. No other creatures, except for seagulls that must have come up from the coast, and now wheeled and skimmed far away, overhead, ignoring her.

In that passage Kate's sense of loneliness, of isolation, is achieved by repetition of the phrase "no people"; and again there were "no other creatures" except for the seagulls who were ignoring her.

Although you should try to make the transition between scenes as smooth as possible, you don't need to walk your characters through every minute of their day. If, for example, you are moving them from one location to another, there's no point in giving an account of their train journey, taxi-ride, or whatever, unless that journey is in itself significant and a vital part of the story. A single sentence is often enough to serve as a bridge from one scene to the next.

The worst sin

To my mind, the worst sin you can commit when writing for children is to be dull. Most children's writers, while hoping their work will inform and enlighten, know that it is unlikely to achieve either of these objectives unless it manages at the same time to be entertaining. On the whole, children have a fairly low threshold of boredom, so any tendency to relapse into stodginess should be sharply knocked on the head.

A lively prose style is essential. This means you must avoid long, complex sentences and the kind of bland, oversimplified language that makes everything you write sound like one continuous cliché. You owe it to your readers to be original, even adventurous, in your use of words. Children are fascinated

40

by language; they are themselves still at the experimental stage, trying out new words every day. That's why you shouldn't be afraid to use the occasional difficult word, provided its meaning is sufficiently clear from the context. I don't know how old I was when I first read Beatrix Potter's *Tale of the Flopsy Bunnies*, but it was the word "soporific" that made the strongest impression on me and I was never in any doubt as to what it meant; similarly the Parsee's "Superior comestible" in Kipling's *Just So Stories*.

Children love to try and unravel mysteries. They love to test out their courage by being a little bit scared. Above all, they love to laugh. If you can introduce humour – natural, not forced – into your stories then you are off to a flying start. Be warned, though, that the humour they enjoy most is pretty basic: anything too subtle will go down like a lead balloon. Whenever I read aloud to children from my own book, *Washington and the Marrow Raiders*, a scene they always seem to enjoy is where the villains, Gordon and Septimus, climb over the garden wall and encounter Grandad Ramage, who is sitting up all night to guard his prize marrow.

Gordon, having landed rather less softly than Septimus in a blackberry bush, was creeping towards the motionless figure of Grandad Ramage. So intent was he on watching for any warning signs of movement that he failed to notice the rake propped up against the garden shed until his foot pressed down the metal teeth and the handle flew up and hit him with considerable force. "Suffering cats! Who did that?" he demanded loudly, momentarily stunned by the impact.

"Eh, what?" Grandad Ramage sat up with a jerk. His eyes went straight to the beam of light hovering over the marrow bed and the shadowy figure crouched behind it. "Here, what's going on?"

"Something to cover his head," muttered Gordon, frantically searching around for an old sack. He found instead a bucket containing potato peelings and eggshells collected from the Whooshamatic for the compost and swiftly upended it over Grandad Ramage.

Finding himself suddenly buried under an avalanche of rubbish

> Grandad Ramage let out a bellow of rage which, amplified by the bucket, sounded almost inhuman, like a wounded elephant.

Shortly afterwards Gordon, while trying to escape over the wall, loses his trousers. Pure slapstick, of course. But it's that element of pantomime that seems to appeal most to children, at least until they reach the age where they become more worldly-wise and selective about what makes them laugh.

The Whooshamatic mentioned above, a machine for dispensing ready-cooked food, is one of Dame Barbara's inventions; and so is the Boomsprocket, a vehicle which runs solely on garden compost. Funny, descriptive names help to make a story memorable – how about the Whipple-Scrumptious Fudgemallow Delight or Cavity-filling Caramels in Roald Dahl's *Charlie and the Chocolate Factory?*

But humour needn't be restricted solely to the more frivolous, lighthearted sort of book. When used skilfully in the treatment of even the most serious subjects it can often restore that sense of balance which is so important when you are writing for children.

To sum up, you can bring your story to life by:
1 Strong, well-rounded characterisation
2 "Making a scene of it"
3 Lively, natural-sounding dialogue
4 Description that conveys mood and emotion
5 An entertaining prose style

4

THE STORY'S THE THING!

Storytelling is an ancient art. The best of the storytellers, like
Homer and Queen Shahrazad, knew exactly how to keep their
listeners on the edge of their seats. Indeed, Shahrazad's life
depended on her ability to do just that. Skilful construction, the
spacing out of climaxes, and knowing exactly the point where
you should leave your readers wanting to know what happens
next – these are the techniques we shall be examining in this
chapter, before going on to look more closely at the type of story
you may wish to write.

Construction

To say that a story will find its own length, and provide its own
clues as to how best it may be constructed, may sound like
wishful thinking; nonetheless, it usually turns out that way. The
average length of a children's novel is between 25,000 and 35,000
words, but some are considerably longer. If you are dealing with
a large subject you will need a large canvas. Conversely, an idea
conceived on a smaller scale could easily be ruined if you try to
blow it up to twice its natural size.

Writing your first chapter will tell you a great deal. Where
does it naturally end? If you are writing for younger children
you'll want to keep the structure fairly simple, perhaps dealing

with only one scene. That's fine, because children like short chapters. Coming to the end of something gives them a sense of achievement. And does it end on a high note or a question mark that will make them want to carry on reading? Then you've probably got it right. What's more, that first chapter will have established the pattern for the rest of the book.

Does this mean that all your chapters have to be the same length? Roughly, yes. There are no hard and fast rules, of course. You may find you have a short but vitally important scene which won't join on comfortably either to the preceding or to the following chapter. In that case it may be more telling if it's isolated. But remember, children like patterns. They need to know where they are with a book, so if you take them by surprise too often they may become irritated and give up altogether.

Take care to space out your high points so that they build up the tension. If you have a long stretch without much happening then perhaps you need to condense that section, or alternatively, introduce some kind of conflict. If you find you have a scene without any conflict at all – even internal – then it's probably best left out altogether. Above all, there must always be a sense of something coming, an interesting development lurking just around the corner.

Try to avoid contrivances. By that I mean devices that are introduced for the purpose of the plot but which don't ring true. In fact this can't happen if you've got inside the skin of your characters, because they will dictate the course of the plot and make it impossible for you to force them into unnatural situations.

Unfortunately coincidences, which occur remarkably often in real life, always seem suspiciously convenient if you put them into a book. Whilst you may be able to get away with using one at the very beginning, so that it acts as the springboard of a story, to introduce one at a later point will look remarkably like contrivance.

Sometimes, I must warn you, there's a period around the

middle of a book where you begin to wonder if you have lost control. In my own mind I term this "middle-aged spread". It happens when the threads running through your story are beginning to proliferate and there's a danger that the piece of cloth you're weaving is losing its shape. I don't know how other writers deal with this, but I suspect they all have different methods. My own is to forge on, trying to keep hold of the most important threads, until eventually I find my way out of the labryinth. Later, when the book is finished, I'll go back to that middle section and re-work it in the light of subsequent development. This is because I find it difficult to see the book as a whole until the final chapter is written. Only then do I have a clear picture of what its shape should be.

Other writers may work quite differently, preferring to get it right before they go any further, and those who have carefully pre-planned their work probably don't have this problem at all. So once again you'll have to find the method that best accords with your own temperament. Whichever way you work, however, be prepared to make several drafts of each chapter, if necessary, until you are satisfied with what you've done.

As for that final chapter, to which your book should be flowing with beautiful inevitability – well, I'm going to make you wait, in the best traditions of storytelling, until after we've considered the kind of story you may choose to write.

What kind of story?

Your choice will largely be dictated by your own tastes and interests. If you enjoy reading mysteries, the chances are that you'll be on the same wavelength as the child who also loves mysteries. If your passion is history then why not try your hand at a historical novel? The greatest mistake you could make would be to choose, say, science fiction because you've heard that it sells well, even though you're only slightly interested in the subject and have little specialist knowledge.

It may be useful to consider some of the main headings under which publishers tend to categorise books. There are, of course, certain books which defy categorisation, so this is not intended to be a definitive list, merely a rough guide; and it deals mainly with books for the middle age range, since those intended for the Under Sevens and Young Adults are dealt with specifically in later chapters. It also excludes fantasy, which demands – and deserves – a chapter to itself.

Animal books

These have always been popular with children. Stories about horses, dogs, cats, deer, bears, even gerbils have found favour over the years, and their hold shows no sign of weakening. There's such a wealth of animal stories available, however, that you need to have something really fresh and lively to offer if you want to break into this field. To write about the real-life adventures of your own pet dog, however amusing they may seem to you, may not strike a publisher as being different enough for him to take a chance on it – unless of course you're Frank Muir writing about What-a-mess.

The irony is that, as soon as a subject is dismissed as "overworked", the chances are that someone will come along and make a nonsense of that statement. Just when everyone had decided there was no more mileage in talking rabbits, along came Richard Adams to prove them wrong by writing *Watership Down*. And although the purists may say that animals should always be depicted behaving as animals do behave and in their natural habitat – ie not wearing funny clothes and living in houses and talking to humans – you have only to see a child devouring the Paddington books to realise that this is being pedantic.

Animal books, therefore, can be divided into two main types: those about real animals acting in a realistic manner – *Black*

Beauty and *Tarka the Otter* are excellent examples of this genre – and those which pretend to be about animals but are in fact about humans in disguise. This last seems to me a perfectly valid form of storytelling, since it enables children to identify with the central character and share his adventures once removed, as it were. In one of the best children's books ever written, E.B. White's *Charlotte's Web*, Wilbur the pig is in grave danger of being slaughtered and is only saved by the ingenuity of Charlotte the spider. This situation could easily be disturbing for children but, although they're naturally concerned for Wilbur, they feel sufficiently distanced by the animal device to be able to cope with it.

Possibly the greatest hazard when writing about animals is that it is all too easy, when describing a small and endearing creature, to lapse into sentimentality. Use of the word "little" seems to constitute a particular danger. "The mouse shed a tear" is one thing; "The mouse shed a *little* tear" quite another.

One kind of animal story whose popularity seems to have declined in recent years is the pony book. The reason, I suspect, is not that there are fewer children interested in horses – in fact there are probably more – but that the genre itself fell into disrepute at one time, owing to the poor quality of some of the writing. At its best, though, it has a lot to offer, as you'll see if you read Mary Treadgold's *We Couldn't Leave Dinah* or Jane Gardam's *Bridget and William*. Provided, therefore, that you're familiar with horses and know your snaffle from your martingale, this could still be a fruitful area to explore.

Fairytale, myth, and legend

Stories about fairies *as such* are not in fashion right now. It may well be that you know children who still lap them up, and of course there's always a chance you'll come up with something so refreshingly different that a publisher will jump at it. Nonetheless, most children over the age of six groan at the mere mention of fairies, elves, and pixies, possibly because they associate them with the nauseatingly twee style of storytelling that used to be thought appropriate. In my opinion, this does a grave injustice to the world of faery; but if you are going to venture into this field I suggest you go back to its roots and try to find a completely new approach.

The re-telling of ancient myths and folk-tales always delights children – no danger of tweeness here – but obviously there's already a wealth of beautifully illustrated books covering the best known areas. If, however, you have a collection of stories from a part of the world which has been less well documented, then it's certainly worth having a go. Or, like Terry Jones with *The Saga of Erik the Viking*, you can invent your own mythological world, which seems authentic but isn't.

The re-telling of myths and folk-tales in a modern form crops up again and again both in adult and in children's literature. The story of Cinderella, for example, is one of the most irresistible plots in the world and the variety of interpretations writers can put upon it is seemingly inexhaustible. So is the Sleeping Beauty. And in *Snow White in New York*, Fiona French tells in fascinating Art Deco pictures how Snow White, having fallen foul of her father's new wife, the Queen of the New York Underworld, finds work as a singer with seven jazzmen. The possibilities seem endless. All you need is a fresh eye.

Mystery and adventure
This is possibly the broadest stream in children's fiction, embracing everything that sets out primarily to tell a thumping good story.

But need it be pure escapism?

At one end of the scale it undoubtedly is, transporting the reader to a world quite outside his own experience, and none the worse for that. As a child I read Arthur Ransome's *Swallows and Amazons* over and over again, revelling in the exploits of children who lived a far more active and independent life than I did. The fact that I knew nothing about sailing and hadn't a clue what cleats and halyards and thwarts were didn't matter one bit. That was all part of the fascination. Escapism it may have been, but I believe it also widened my horizons.

When writing a mystery you start with an enormous advantage, since most children love the puzzle element in a story and can't resist the challenge of trying to solve it. This is the kind of book where it probably helps if you're a pre-planner, because you really do need to be very organised when it comes to planting vital clues and red herrings throughout the plot, always keeping one step ahead of your reader.

It seems to me that a distinction should be made between mystery and crime since, when writing crime stories, you inevitably run into practical difficulties as soon as your child characters become involved with dangerous criminals. These may, of course, be comic criminals; but if they are in any way realistic it can be difficult to make the children's ultimate victory over them believable. To have the police take over in the last chapter, charging to the rescue like the US cavalry, is a terrible let-down. So is the discovery that the mysterious wooden box everyone has been making such a fuss about contains the inevitable cache of stolen jewels or bank-notes or contraband. Far more interesting, to my mind, are mysteries about *people* – why they lie and cheat and occasionally act in a way that seems entirely out of character. If there's a crime involved, then let it be understandable in human terms and not merely a device of the plot.

Perhaps the chief danger in this particular genre is the temptation to devise the plot first and put the characters in later. This inevitably results in weak characterisation; and although children may still read and enjoy the story, it won't make the lasting impression on them that a more fully conceived book would have done.

Historical novels
It is often said that historical novels don't sell well these days

because children are more interested in the future than they are in the past. Well, there may be some truth in that. But it is interesting to note that some of the most talented and prestigious writers of children's fiction are to be found in this field – Geoffrey Trease, Rosemary Sutcliffe, Leon Garfield, Henry Treece, and Jill Paton Walsh among others.

They are, of course, all highly intelligent, articulate writers, and it is inevitable that their books appeal primarily to highly intelligent, articulate children. This seems to me to be only fair and just. These days, thank goodness, a great many books are produced specifically to suit the less able child, but we shouldn't forget that the exceptionally bright and able reader also needs to be catered for. So if you should decide to write a historical novel you'll find a select but appreciative readership awaiting you.

This readership, however, is used to – and therefore has come to expect – only the best. It is no use thinking that, just because you're writing for children, you can skimp on research. A child who is interested in history may well have acquired a phenomenal knowledge of his particular period and will be quick to spot any kind of inaccuracy. Geoffrey Trease has this cautionary tale to tell:

> In *Mist Over Athelney*, when I realised that my adventurous young people would have to eat sooner or later, I let them encounter a hermit and share his campfire supper of rabbit stew. That detail passed my learned publishers without comment; it passed the *Times Literary Supplement* and a host of other reviewers. But it didn't pass an eleven-year-old boy in Aberdeen, who wrote to tell me that there were no rabbits in England before the Norman Conquest.
>
> *Children's Literature in Education*, no. 7, March 1972

Dialogue in historical novels can present a problem. Obviously you want to avoid relapsing into the odds-bodikins-stap-me-vitals school of language. But should you try as far as possible to reproduce the authentic speech of the period, or is it safer to settle for contemporary, idiomatic English?

Somewhere between the two is probably the best answer. In fact it would be a near-impossibility to reproduce authentic Anglo-Saxon, for example, and if you did it would be incomprehensible to your readers. Far better to write dialogue that sounds natural to modern ears, while avoiding the use of jarring anachronisms. Remember, nothing must get in the way of the reader's enjoyment, whether it is archaic dialogue he can't follow or a glaringly obtrusive piece of modern slang.

School stories

Publishers, we are told, are crying out for school stories, so why aren't more people writing them?

One theory is that the old favourites – Billy Bunter, Jennings, Stalky & Co – succeeded because they were set in boarding schools, which had the distinct advantage of being closed communities where adults hardly intruded, apart from a few cranky or despotic schoolmasters. Nowadays, although boarding schools still flourish, they have fallen out of favour on elitist grounds, so writers are generally discouraged from setting stories in them.

Admittedly, with a story set in a day school, there's always a danger of the situation losing momentum when the bell goes at four o'clock; and again those wretched parents can get in the way of the plot if you're not careful. But the fact that life goes on outside the school gates can be made to work for you; and so can the parents, provided they are fully realised characters and not mere cyphers. If you are a parent yourself you probably have a pretty good idea what goes on in schools today; and if you're a teacher, even better. It shouldn't be too difficult to put yourself on the other side of the fence. A school is a microcosm, where children experience many of the joys and perplexities they will have to cope with in adult life. It provides a situation rich in possibilities for conflict, humour, and self-discovery. Children are fascinated by it because it so closely concerns themselves. Look at the success of *Grange Hill*.

Remember, though, that this is a field in which all children are experts. So be sure you get your facts right, and strive for the ring of authenticity that will make your story credible.

Ghost and horror

Testing our resistance to fear is a part of growing up. From the Grimm brothers onwards, gruesome tales have always held a particular fascination for the young. It is essential, of course, that they should be viewed from a safe vantage point. We all know of the child who hides behind the sofa when *Dr Who* is on television, daring himself to peer round occasionally and take a look. But if you suggested he shouldn't watch at all he'd be deeply insulted.

Many ghost and horror books come in the form of collections of short stories, perhaps because it is difficult to sustain credibility in anything longer. Some of these have a strangely dated feel about them; and some seem not to have been written for children at all, so that if you read them aloud you're forced to skip the stodgy bits in order to keep the pace going. There are, of course, some excellent anthologies available, but most of them contain stories commissioned from established writers, so it is not an easy field for a novice to break into.

There seems to be far more scope when it comes to book-length ghost stories, and as this is a popular genre publishers are always on the lookout for new material. It is advisable, though, to avoid the cliché situation, such as old haunted houses and dismembered green hands playing the piano at midnight. Humorous ghost stories are welcomed, and if you can make them scary as well so much the better. Some imaginative modern writers have managed to find the most surprising twists to an old theme. Diana Wynne Jones, in *The Time of the Ghost*, tells of four sisters, one of whom discovers that she's become a ghost after a fatal accident. But whose ghost is she? And when did the accident happen – or has it not yet happened?

When it comes to horror the question always arises, How far

should you go? Where do you draw the line between permissible nastiness and what is likely to be genuinely disturbing? Perhaps it is worth bearing in mind that most people are far more scared of the Unknown, the unseen horror in the dark, than by what they can see. In *Dr Who* the monsters are at their most frightening when they're invisible, a threatening presence just outside the door, but as soon as they appear with all their crinkly plastic skin and bulging foreheads they are just plain ludicrous. It's the anticipation that makes the child hide behind the sofa, not the reality.

Clearly, though, you have a moral obligation here, especially when writing for younger children. In the end Good must be shown to triumph over Evil, Light over Dark. That is the certainty which makes it possible for a child to test his courage, secure in his belief that the world is basically an orderly, benevolent place. If this goes against the artistic grain, then perhaps you should be writing horror stories for adults, not children.

Humour

Although humour can be found in all categories, especially fantasy, there is an area where it exists in its own right. I'm thinking particularly of *Just William*, as well as the *Ramona* stories of Beverley Cleary and Dorothy Edward's *My Naughty Little Sister*. These are all collections of stories about children with whom any normal, grubby-kneed, accident-prone child can identify. They are often farcical, but never slip over the edge into whimsy. Moreover they have a freshness and vitality about them that doesn't seem to date, and which no doubt accounts for their continued popularity. If you have a well-developed sense of the ridiculous, and take pleasure in making people laugh, you may well find this a fruitful area to explore.

The final chapter

Someone once said to me that the final chapter of a children's book is rather like the grand finale of a pantomine – everyone assembled on stage, revealed at last in their true colours, to take their farewell bow. It depends, of course, on the type of book you're writing, but certainly there should be some kind of grand climax, a drawing together of threads, that will send your audience away happy and contented that they've had their money's worth.

Drawing up the threads, however, and tying them in a satisfying knot, can be a tricky business. What you must avoid at all costs is a scene akin to the *dénouement* in the old-style detective novel, where the Inspector gathers together all the suspects in the drawing-room and holds forth for several pages of lengthy explanation about who did what and why. Ideally, the reader should have been made aware as the story unfolded exactly why the characters acted as they did, so that by the time you reach the final chapter there's no need to analyse everyone's motives. Action, not explanation, is what children are hoping for at the end of a story – the grand bust-up, with the hero triumphant and the villain getting his come-uppance.

For older readers, of course, this can be done with more subtlety. It is possible, even desirable, to leave at least one thread untied, one question unanswered, so that they can draw their own conclusions. The reaction that you, as the writer, are hoping for is the long drawn-out sigh of satisfaction. Of course – that's how it *had* to end! But at the same time you want the reader to feel that the characters will go on with their lives after the book is closed.

Be careful, too, that you finish immediately you have nothing important left to say. Once, to my shame, an editor had to cut the final two paragraphs of my book because I'd let it drag on beyond its natural conclusion. Rather like seeing someone off at a railway station, if the train doesn't move out on time your

smile becomes fixed and your waves mechanical.
So when you come to the end – stop.

5

THE PROFESSIONAL TOUCH

At last your story is finished! You've put the final full stop to the final sentence and now you can't wait to send it off to a publisher.

WAIT!

Don't be too hasty. This is the stage that separates the professional from the novice and may well be the deciding factor as to whether or not your story will sell. It is time to rest, recharge your batteries, and take a long cool look at what you've done so far.

A critical eye

The first thing you need to do is distance yourself from your work. At the moment you're probably still flushed with the excitement of creation: euphoria has set in and you're convinced you've produced the best children's book since *Treasure Island*. That's only to be expected. If you weren't passionately in love with what you were doing you wouldn't have had the energy to write it. Now you need to be more objective.

I recommend that you put it away in a drawer and forget about it for at least a week, preferably longer. Do something entirely different, such as gardening, playing the violin or catching up on all the housework you've neglected while you were writing. Not until your mind is clear and you feel quite calm and detached about the whole thing are you ready to take your manuscript out of the drawer and settle down to read it with a critical eye.

Has it turned out exactly as you intended?

Well, it may have done, if you happen to be one of those rare people whose minds are so well-organised that they get it right first time. But the chances are that on re-reading your work you'll find a lot of rough edges, some sentences that could have been better constructed, and whole passages in need of drastic cutting and re-shaping. In which case it's far better to revise it *now*, before it goes off to a publisher, than send it half-finished and hope he won't notice there's anything wrong.

There is a school of thought that says too much revision can destroy the natural spontaneity of a book, and of course that's the last thing you want. It depends how you interpret the word "revision". In fact what you're aiming to do is iron out all the awkward phrases and clumsy bits of construction so that the book reads smoothly and effortlessly, giving the *illusion* of spontaneity. Therein lies the whole art of writing.

In order to revise your work you have to be ruthlessly self-critical; but before you can start criticising you need to know what the weaknesses are that you are looking for.

Here are some questions you should ask yourself:

1 *Does the story get off to a good start?*
Look again at that all-important first chapter. Is the opening arresting enough? Will it catch a young reader's attention?

2 *Are there any dull bits?*
Check for stodge. You may be surprised to find how long a particular scene goes on without much happening. If necessary, be prepared to cut large chunks of introspection or superfluous dialogue.

3 *Have I made everything clear?*

Maybe you've left out some vital piece of information, assuming that the reader will understand what's happening without being told. Or possibly you'll find a sentence that even you have to read twice before you can make sense of it, so pity the poor reader.

4 *Have I used too many adjectives and adverbs?*

Almost certainly. It's a fault most writers have to guard against, the compulsion to qualify nouns and verbs in case they don't have enough impact. Perhaps you can choose other nouns or verbs that are strong enough to stand alone.

5 *Have I been self-indulgent?*

In any book there are always certain passages – usually descriptive – of which you are inordinately fond, but which may be totally irrelevant. Or you may have expounded at some length on a subject you feel particularly strongly about, thereby lapsing into preachiness. Or you may have crammed in too many facts and figures rather than waste all that interesting research. If so, cut them out.

6 *Does it flow well?*

A writer's sense of euphony, his awareness of whether or not a sentence has the right rhythm and achieves a satisfying counter-point with what goes before and after, is largely a matter of instinct. If you are uncertain, try reading your work aloud, preferably to somebody else. This often helps you to spot any jarring notes or clumsy transitions.

7 *Have I checked all my references?*

This is very important. Memory can play the strangest tricks and even facts you're certain you know can turn out to be wrong. You can't afford to take anything for granted. It is possible, of course, that if you make a mistake it will be picked up by the editor working on your book; but if you make too many he won't have a very high opinion of your reliability as an author. So check and double-check all your facts.

8 *Have I chosen an appealing title?*
A child choosing a book from the library shelf will be drawn partly by the title and partly by the jacket. You may not have much control over the jacket design, but you can make sure that your title contains words that catch his eye and fire his imagination, while at the same time giving him some idea of what the book is about.

You may feel, when you have finished revising your work, that you'd like to try reading it aloud to a child or class of children and ask for their opinions. This can be a helpful exercise, especially when it comes to spotting where the dull bits are – yawns and shuffling feet are the danger signs – but be warned that the comments you receive are not likely to be very constructive. If children like you they'll tell you what they think you want to hear; and even if they say frankly there were parts of it they didn't enjoy, they probably won't be able to tell you why.

Writers' Circles

This brings me to the question of whether or not you would find it helpful to join a Writer's Circle.

If you are lucky enough to have a practical Writers' Circle near to where you live, then I would unhesitatingly advise you to join it. By "practical" I mean one where the members meet frequently to consider each other's work and make constructive comments. Taking criticism is never easy and often I find myself resisting it strongly; but if several people make the same comment there's a good chance they're right. In any case you'll have to show your work eventually to a highly critical publisher, so you may as well get in a little early practice at taking it on the chin.

Often, too, a fresh eye can spot inconsistencies you are incapable of seeing yourself because you're too close. Once I read to my Writers' Group a chapter about a girl and a boy who were lost in the mist on Dartmoor. As it drew near the end one member's expression grew more and more puzzled. When I'd finished he said, "Fine – but what happened to the dog?" I'd been so carried away writing about the girl and boy that I'd completely forgotten about their dog, even though I'd clearly stated that he was with them when they left home. Can you imagine how agitated children would become, reading the book, if they thought – quite wrongly – that the dog had been abandoned on the moors in a swirling mist?

Incidentally, never feel you must preface reading out your work with a humble, "I'm afraid this is only a children's story". Most people can appreciate a good story at any level. In any case, writing for children is not, as we've seen, something for which you need to apologise.

Presentation

It may be true to say that, if you have written a masterpiece, a publisher will overlook the fact that it's badly typed on scruffy paper and full of spelling mistakes. Provided, that is, he isn't so put off by its appearance that he refuses to read it! Admittedly looks aren't everything, but a weary editor will almost certainly choose to take home a clean, well-presented manuscript to read in preference to a near-illegible one.

The final copy should be clearly typed on one side only of good quality A4 paper. Use double spacing throughout, with no extra spaces between paragraphs. All pages must be numbered either in the centre or at the top right-hand corner; and you should leave good margins all round, but especially on the left-hand side. Keep last-minute alterations to a minimum; and if you must change something do so neatly and clearly. The front page should contain only the title, the author's name, address, and telephone number, and the approximate number of words.

If you are not a particularly good typist it is well worth paying to have your manuscript typed professionally. If you do it yourself on a manual typewriter take care to change the ribbon whenever it's getting faint. And if, like me, you use a word processor with a dot matrix printer, make sure that the print-out is clear and not so "dotty" that it's difficult to read. This may necessitate using near letter quality throughout, depending on your printer. If you have a daisy-wheel printer, of course, this won't be a problem.

Spelling mistakes, in my opinion, aren't a mortal sin: nonetheless it's preferable not to make them. If you know you're a poor speller, have a dictionary constantly on hand; and ask someone else to check your work before you send it off, just in case.

Punctuation is always tricky because it can vary so much according to fashion and also to geography: American punctuation, for example, differs slightly from our own. In fact it was my American editor who cured me of my addiction to dots and dashes. When writing dialogue I used to end practically every speech with either a dash or three dots to indicate that this was an ongoing conversation. Not only was this unnecessary, it was also distracting for the reader. She also made me aware how often I used exclamation marks when, strictly speaking, they weren't needed. Unfortunately, it's all too easy to get into bad habits, which you don't even notice until someone points them out to you. If you are uncertain about punctuation, the best thing to do is look at a published book to see how somebody else has dealt with the problem.

Illustrations

Is it a good idea to provide your own?

If you are a professional artist with experience in the field of illustration, yes. If not, I'm afraid there's very little chance that a publisher will use them. Even if you have an artistic friend who has offered to do some drawings to accompany your text, it is unlikely that they'd be acceptable. Nearly all publishers prefer to put their work in the hands of the tried and true illustrators with whom their editors are used to working.

I must admit that I've always been deeply envious of those writers who are able to illustrate their own work. To have such complete control over the final product must be immensely satisfying. Even so, my greatest thrill – next to hearing that my first book had been accepted – came when I received the illustrations through the post and saw how the artist had brought my characters to life. They were astonishingly close to my original conception, but the artist had added something extra from her own highly visual imagination, so that the final result was more fully realised than would otherwise have been possible.

Picture books, of course, are a different matter, as are the illustrations for educational books, and these will be dealt with in subsequent chapters.

Sending your "baby" out into the world

Now comes the moment you've been both longing for and dreading, when you pack up your precious manuscript and send it off.

First make sure you keep at least one copy, preferably two. It is not unknown for manuscripts to be lost in the post or mislaid in some publisher's office. And the thought of having to write a book twice is unthinkable.

Should you send it straight to a publisher or try to find an agent?

A good agent will advise you on your work, send it out to publishers he knows are looking for the type of book you've written, and – if you are lucky enough to be accepted – negotiate on your behalf the terms of the contract. Unfortunately these days it can be more difficult to find an agent than it is to find a publisher. However, most publishers say that it makes no difference whether your work comes to them direct or is filtered through an agent. If it's good, they'll sit up and take notice. And when it comes to negotiating your own contract, if you write to the Society of Authors at 84 Drayton Gardens, London SW10 9SD they may, for a small fee, let you have a copy of their guide to authors on this subject. Once you are a published writer you'll be eligible to join the Society, whose members are entitled to have their contracts vetted free.

To answer the original question, you've nothing to lose by trying one or two agents first; if they show no interest then you can start writing to publishers.

How do you go about finding one?

Names and addresses of agents and publishers are given in the *Writers' and Artists' Year Book*. Selecting an agent is difficult, unless you happen to hear of one who's specially recommended. This is where it helps if you belong to a Writers' Circle or go to one of the Writers' Workshops or Conferences that may be organised in your area. You can pick up all sorts of useful information that way. When it comes to finding a publisher, you need to do your market research. Look in bookshops and libraries to see which publishing houses specialise in the kind of book you have to offer. You may be able to make quite a long list, and then it's a matter of working your way steadily through them.

Should you send a letter first?

Yes. It is quite possible that a publisher's fiction list may be closed for the time being, so there's no point in wasting his time and your postage by sending the complete manuscript until you know he's prepared to read it. Make the letter as brief and business-like as possible – ie don't give him your entire life history and your views on writing in general – but enclose a short synopsis of the story and possibly your curriculum vitae if you think it's relevant. I always think it's a good idea to send a copy of the first chapter as well, because this will give a far better idea of your writing skill than a brief synopsis. And don't forget to enclose a stamped addressed envelope for their reply.

How should you package it?

This may sound a little unnerving, but it seems that publishers prefer manuscripts that come in the form of loose pages. They don't like pins or staples and aren't particularly keen on MSS that are clamped into a file. Paper clips are okay, provided they're the flat variety that don't get caught up in other documents. What I usually do is use paper clips to separate the chapters and place the entire manuscript, provided it's slim enough, inside an envelope folder. If it's too bulky for that I put it into a box – the kind in which typing paper comes is ideal. And if it's still too bulky, then I take a deep breath and remove the paper clips, so that it can lie flat. Yes, I know it sounds risky, especially if a sudden gust of wind should blow through the window while someone is reading your manuscript, but as long as you've remembered to number your pages it shouldn't be too disastrous.

Again, don't forget to send stamps to cover the cost of return postage. And if you want to be certain they acknowledge the safe arrival of your manuscript, send a stamped postcard for them to despatch as soon as they've received it.

How long should you wait for a decision?

Three months is the average "waiting time". After that you either start getting extremely hopeful or begin to wonder if they've lost it; but you're afraid of upsetting them – possibly at the crucial moment of decision – by demanding that they send your manuscript back. Take comfort: this is a dilemma all writers experience. In fact, after three months you'd be perfectly justified in writing politely to ask if they've come to a decision yet. It may jolt their memories and is very unlikely to put them off if they're genuinely enthusiastic about your book.

Is it permissible to send your manuscript to more than one publisher at the same time?

Permissible, yes. But is it advisable? At one time this practice was frowned upon, because of the danger that more than one publisher might be interested, which meant that whichever one you turned down would not take a very kindly view of your work in the future. These days, however, it's quite common for agents to send a manuscript to several publishers at once in order to introduce an element of competition. This may be all right for an agent, or even for an established author, but I think a novice would be best advised to stick to the accepted code of practice. If for some reason you need to accelerate the speed of submissions, then approach the publishers by letter but make it clear that you are writing similar letters to other publishers. It may work, depending on the nature of what you have to offer, but generally speaking you'll make a better impression if you concentrate on one publisher at a time.

On bouncing back

Less welcome, even, than an electricity bill or an income tax demand is the sight of your returned manuscript coming through the letter box. You are allowed about half-an-hour of suicidal gloom, after which you have to remind yourself that many successful books have been rejected, some as many as 26 times, and yet have gone on to be best-sellers. Obviously *their* authors didn't sit around and mope!

Before sending it out again, however, it is worth taking another look at it, even at this stage, especially if the publisher has made any comment. He may say, for example, that it started well but he found the end disappointing. If, on reflection, you decide that he could be right, you'd be well advised to try to improve the end before sending it out again. The fact that he's made any comment at all should be regarded as encouraging: at least he hasn't sent it back to you with a printed rejection slip.

This ability to "bounce back" after a rejection requires strength of character. It would be only too easy to give up what often appears to be a hopelessly unequal struggle, trying to get your book published against all the odds. Nobody, it seems, wants to know; they are obviously blind to your qualities as a writer, so what's the point of going on? This is where the real test comes. Are you determined enough to go on until you break through the publication barrier?

. When students first come along to my Creative Writing classes, I am often amazed at how talented some of them are, producing work that deserves to be read by a wider public. The fact is, though, that talent alone is not enough: it's the ones who have talent *plus* stickability who will eventually succeed in getting something published. Paradoxically, a writer has to develop a certain toughess if he's to survive in the highly commercial world of publishing, while at the same time retaining the sensitivity that is essential to his work. It isn't that he doesn't care when he's rejected; it's simply that he won't take "no" for an answer – at least, not until he has exhausted all possible outlets.

It's true, of course, that luck plays quite a large part in deciding whether or not your book is accepted. It has to land on the right desk at the right time; everything depends on the editor being on your wavelength. What a gamble!

But that's what gets the adrenalin going. There's always the chance that tomorrow the telephone will ring and someone will say, "We like this book. Can you come and talk to us about it?" And if THAT happens it'll probably take a lot longer than half-an-hour for you to come down from Cloud Nine.

On being flexible

What may bring you back to earth with a bump is the discovery that the editor wants you to make some alterations.

Your initial instinct will be to clutch your manuscript protectively to your chest and say, "No, I don't want to change a thing. I like it just the way it is." My advice is to murmur something non-committal and go home to think about it. The chances are that you'll come round to the editor's way of thinking and realise that the changes will be for the better. If, however, you disagree strongly then you must say so, as tactfully as possible, and give your reasons. Once, before commissioning a book, my editor asked me if I could set the story in a different location. I said yes, I could; but it would be an entirely different story and I explained why. She wrote back at once to say that she saw exactly what I meant and please leave the story as it was. I must say, though, that was about the only occasion I can remember when I did raise an objection: usually I try to be as flexible as possible, even if it means having to compromise. That doesn't mean you need sacrifice your principles; only that it's unwise to create difficulties over small, unimportant points, thereby earning yourself a reputation as a "difficult author".

One of the trickiest areas of flexibility is over the jacket design. As I said above, you may not have much say in the matter, although most editors will send a copy at some stage for your approval – usually when it's too late for you to object! If your book is coming out in hardback, it's a good idea to ask if you can see a "rough" of the jacket before the block is made, so that you have time to spot any glaring inconsistencies. So often you hear stories of artists getting it wrong, such as showing a girl with fair hair when the text states clearly that she is dark. My US publishers have the whole thing very well organised: as soon as the book is accepted, they ask the author to fill in detailed art facts sheets, giving full physical descriptions of the main characters together with suggestions as to what kind of situation you would like illustrated on the jacket. Not all publishers are so open to suggestion, but if you do have an idea about the jacket design then you should mention it early on in your discussions, rather than waiting until it's too late for alterations. There's no guarantee they'll take it up, but if it's good they'll certainly bear it in mind.

Remember, the relationship you form with your editor is going to be of vital importance, not only where your first book is concerned but also in the way it affects your future work. Your writing career doesn't end with the publication of your first book. On the contrary, it has only just begun.

6

WRITING FOR THE UNDER-SEVENS

Babies Need Books is the title of Dorothy Butler's comprehensive study, based on her belief that "books can be used not only to entertain and to comfort, but also to stimulate the imagination, to stir the emotions and to help the early forging of relationships". Children who have access to books at an early age are likely to regard them as friends and companions for the rest of their lives; whereas children deprived of books may well see them as alien tools, even instruments of torture, when they first encounter them on starting school.

Writing for the under-sevens is therefore a worthwhile – and an enjoyable – occupation. Be warned, though, that it's not as easy as it looks. I've seen people flip through a picture book with only a few words on each page and mutter, "Good heavens, anyone could do this. It must be money for old rope!" In fact the simplicity is deceptive. Like an iceberg with only the tip showing, there's a lot going on beneath the surface.

A world of wonder and delight

If you are a parent or a grandparent or even a godparent, you are no doubt well acquainted with the amazing quality and range of books available today for small children. They include board books, pop-up books, finger games, nursery rhymes, bedtime stories, alphabet books and activity books as well as every story theme you can think of. There seems no end to the inventiveness of authors like Eric Carle, whose *Very Hungry Caterpillar* almost literally eats his way through the pages of the book; or Janet and Allan Ahlberg, whose *Jolly Postman* delivers a postbag of real letters which children can open up and read.

So how on earth do you find a fresh approach?

Well, for a start you can try to avoid climbing on somebody else's bandwagon. After the publication of Jan Pienkowski's magical *Haunted House* the market was flooded with similar publications, most of them inferior; and one editor told me that the number of imitation *Postman Pat* books she'd been sent was unbelievable. Much the same goes for *Paddington* and *Thomas the Tank Engine*.

If, however, you take a closer look at what's on offer you may come to some interesting conclusions.

What kind of book?

The first discovery you make will probably be that books for this age group fall into two distinct categories: those intended to be read aloud by an adult and those designed for children to read by themselves. Of these two categories the first is by far the largest: in fact it is only quite recently that publishers have woken up to the fact that there is a real need for first reading books.

In both categories, of course, the story is of primary importance. And I use the word "story" intentionally, since although some of the simplest books may seem to have a theme rather than a plot, if you look at them closely you will see that there's still a progression of ideas towards a satisfying conclusion. They follow a pattern; and this is the age when patterns are not only desirable, but of paramount importance.

Almost anything, whether animate or inanimate, can be the

central character in a children's book. Val Biro's *Gumdrop* is a vintage car; Leo Leonni's *Little Blue and Little Yellow* are two blobs of colour who play together and eventually become one green blob. Stories about animals abound, of course; but my local children's librarian often bemoans the fact that, when she wants something to read aloud to groups of small children, all she can find are books about mice and kittens and ducks. "I wish I could find more books that look at the world from a child's viewpoint," she says.

Shirley Hughes is a writer who manages brilliantly to do just that. Her stories show small children against an easily recognisable family background, coping with the sort of problems that small children have to cope with, such as going to live in a new neighbourhood in *Moving Molly*, or the loss of a dearly loved toy in *Dogger*. Even something as simple as a burst pipe can form the basis of an Alfie adventure in *An Evening at Alfie's*. She says: "Picture books are a very good way of having a dialogue with a child. I'm simply amazed by the way children can take a story and make it their own, using it as a way of reinforcing their own experience of life as well as a starting point for their own stories and pictures".

Pictures plus words

Looking at the work of Shirley Hughes brings us face to face with a major consideration when it comes to writing for this age range, since she both writes and illustrates her books. In fact she started her professional life as an illustrator and only later discovered that writing the words as well gave her a satisfying degree of control over the finished product.

The relationship between pictures and words, at this level, is clearly very close indeed. If you are an imaginative writer *and* a gifted artist you start with an enormous advantage: but if you

71

happen to be one and not the other, then your best hope is to find a partner whose skills perfectly complement your own. It is possible that an idea you submit to a publisher may appeal to him so strongly that he will act as matchmaker. After all, he is far more likely to know of possible authors or illustrators than you are. If you are an author, I'm afraid that selecting an artist whose work you like and writing to them care of their publishers may not be the best approach. The chances are that, if they are already well-established, they'll have a full workload for many months to come. One possible solution is to keep an eye on the work produced by students who've specialised in illustration at art school; a stroll around a leavers' exhibition may well prove fruitful.

Whether or not you're an author-and-artist combined or just an author, the main requirement is that you should be able to *think* in pictures. This may sound obvious: in fact it demands a totally different technique from any other form of storytelling. Once I was asked to supply the ideas for a series of stories told entirely in pictures. Great! I thought; no words at all – that'll be a piece of cake. In fact it turned out to be the hardest thing I've ever attempted.

If you look at some picture books for the very young and try to imagine the text – sometimes only a few words to a page – without the pictures, you will realise that it can't be done. The real quality of the book lies in the combination of words *and* pictures, which together form a cohesive whole. Even though it may be the visual image that makes the greatest impact, the illustration can only exist as part of the original concept, which came from the author of the book – and I use the word "author" in the sense of originator. The words may be simple – the concept anything but.

If you divorced the text from the pictures of one of my favourite books, *Princess Smartypants* by Babette Cole, you'd get a very odd idea of the story. For example, when the text states that Princess Smartypants asked one of her suitors, Prince

Rushforth, to feed her pets, it's not until you look at the picture that you realise her "pets" are all fearsome prehistoric monsters. And when the text tells us that she suggested to Prince Fetlock that "he might like to put her pony through its paces", the picture shows the pony kicking up its heels and the Prince sailing through the air. Clearly the lesson to be learned is that you, as author, cannot simply write down a story and hand it over for someone else to illustrate. You must first visualise it as a whole and get it clear in your mind how words and pictures can be made to work together.

Ideally, the world depicted in the illustrations will be rich in possibilities for exploration. In Thomas and Wanda Zacharias's book *But Where is the Green Parrot?* every picture shows the green parrot camouflaged somewhere amidst the foliage, becoming more and more difficult to find as the book progresses. In Pat Hutchins' *Rosie's Walk*, now a modern classic, Rosie the hen takes a seemingly innocent walk through the farmyard, but children listening to the story will be able to spot for themselves the fox who's waiting to pounce on her. Here the words and pictures are working in tandem, but are not both doing the same job.

You will also, of course, need plenty of action. There's a temptation, when you first begin, to tell the story in slowly moving stages like the frames of an animated cartoon. In fact each picture should be complete in itself and contain a "happening": you don't need to show us your characters walking from one scene to the next.

Layout of a picture book

The number of pages in a picture book is governed by the way the paper is folded and can therefore be 16, 24, 32, or 48. Allowing for the fact that the first two pages may be taken up with titles etc, this leaves you with 14, 22, 30, or 46 to play with. If you want to have a few double-page spreads, remember that they must always start with an even-numbered page; eg pp 10 and 11. This may seem so obvious as to be hardly worth mentioning, but it is something I had to learn the hard way.

It is a good idea to work out a rough plan by writing the number of pages down one side of a piece of paper, leaving plenty of room to describe each picture. Be prepared to play about with it a lot before you get the balance right. Your first attempt will almost certainly be either too long or too short.

What happens next depends entirely on how accomplished an artist you are. If you are intending to do your own illustrations, then you should complete two or three to send out as samples of your work, accompanied by a fair copy of your text and a brief description of the concept as a whole. If you prefer to complete all the illustrations before sending it out, so much the better: it depends how much time you have and how confident you are of acceptance. But a publisher will be able to tell from your samples whether or not your work is likely to be of interest to him.

If you are the author and have not yet found an illustrator to work with, then you should present your text and concept as clearly as possible. There's no need to show the layout of words on each page unless there's something unusual about it which it is vital to demonstrate.

Rhythm, rhyme, and repetition

These are the basic three Rs when it comes to writing for small children. In books that are designed for reading aloud by an adult, there are no real limitations as far as vocabulary is concerned since any difficult words can be explained by the reader; nonetheless the choice of words – and their arrangement on the page – is of major importance. In the discipline it imposes on the writer it is rather like writing poetry: the fewer the words you use the more crucial it becomes to get them right.

As these stories are intended to be read aloud, it helps if you have a natural ear for the rhythms of speech. The language you use needn't necessarily be simple, but it should be direct. Avoid falling into the trap of using phrases such as "Up went the fox" and "Down goes she", which employ the kind of syntax no child is likely to encounter in everyday life. But don't be afraid to introduce the odd eccentric, even newly-invented word, especially if it's onomatopoeic, such as the "rumpeta, rumpeta, rumpeta" of the elephant running down the road in Elfrida Vipont's *The Elephant and the Bad Baby*.

Taking rhythm one stage further, we shouldn't overlook the possibility of telling stories in verse. Children love anything that rhymes: again, it implies the existence of a pattern, which is both satisfying and reassuring. Best of all, they love quirky rhymes. Charlotte Hough, in her delightful book *Verse and Various*, now sadly out of print, writes:

> Got a tortoise, name of Torty.
> Torty's ponderously sporty.
> When I lie upon the bank
> He walks across me like a tank.

I defy both child and adult to read that without smiling at the picture it conjures up. And how about that word "ponderously"? Well, can you think of a better one?

"Please will you read it again?" is the best accolade any book can receive. Some stories, it seems, hold an endless fascination for small readers and they never tire of hearing them. This is because they find the familiar reassuring; and repetition within the story itself helps to reinforce that sense of security, as well as building up the tension as the story nears its climax. In John Burningham's *Mr Gumpy's Outing*, Mr Gumpy takes his boat out on the river and is joined by a procession of different creatures, including children, a sheep, a rabbit, and a goat. To each one he affably gives instructions not to muck about too much, while all the time the boat is becoming more and more dangerously overloaded. The ending is inevitable – but not of course disastrous.

First reading books

These are designed for children who have just begun to read alone, so the target age range is roughly from about four to seven-plus. They vary in length from around 1,000 to 5,000 words and are usually lavishly illustrated, forming a bridge between the picture book and the full-length children's novel. For that reason publishers are looking for stories with a strong visual element, using the kind of lively subject matter likely to appeal to contemporary children.

Although they must be easy-to-read, there are no particular restrictions as to vocabulary. The narrative style should be imaginative but simple, with one clear thread which a slow, painstaking reader can grasp and hang on to, no matter how long it takes him to finish the story. Above all, it should be exciting, with the kind of tension that will make him want to persist until he reaches the end.

If you do your market research on First Readers you'll find that many come in the form of series of books, most of which will have been commissioned from writers with a proven track record. Don't let this put you off. There's still plenty of room for more stories of this kind, as any parent or bookseller or librarian will confirm.

One word of warning: when writing for this age group we are usually at pains to create a fictional world that is safe, friendly, and comforting. Unfortunately the real world is very different; and it is therefore necessary to avoid any situation where children talk to strangers, go for walks with them, or accept a lift in a car. This can be a restriction; but you can't afford to take any risks that may endanger the life of a child.

Other options

Living as we do in a technological age, the forward-looking writer of children's stories can't help wondering if there may be options open to him other than the book world. Sadly, it seems that nearly all producers of TV programmes, films, or cassettes prefer to use work that has already been published, rather than take a risk on something original. *Jackanory*, for example, uses very little unpublished material, and even that is usually commissioned from established writers.

The BBC's *Play School*, however, still has a story in every programme. Greg Childs, one of the current producers, writes:

> It is aimed at children from 3 to 5 years, so many of the stories have a practical everyday theme, though elements of fantasy occur too. In *Play School* stories are presented in a variety of ways. Sometimes the presenters, with an extra guest perhaps, "act out" the story, though it remains narrated, more or less. One of the most satisfying forms storytelling takes in *Play School* is when a presenter simply tells the tale to the camera – ie directly to the child viewer. On occasion a few props or hats might be used. A good story told this way is an involving and very direct piece of television.
>
> Stories tend to be around 4 minutes in length. There is no restriction on the use of language or sophistication of ideas, though an awareness of the duration of the tale and the age group it's aimed at is obviously needed.

Christine Hewitt, who is the present series producer, points out that *Play School* has always been concerned to achieve in its storytelling a clear distinction between fantasy and reality, as ambiguity in this area can lead to confusion at the younger end of the age range. It is assumed that children watch alone, without the guidance of a parent or teacher to help them understand the relationship between the fantastic and the real. Certain stories where fantasy and reality are blended may be considered unacceptable for this reason.

Animated series are also occasionally commissioned from outside scriptwriters, but clearly you need to have some knowledge of the technique involved.

The advice given by both the BBC and the IBA companies is to watch their current programmes. It would obviously be pointless to bombard them with ideas that simply don't fit in with a department's overall policy. If you want more information, I suggest you write to BBC Publications for a copy of their handbook *Writing for the BBC*.

7

YOUNG ADULTS

The young adult market, we are told, is a major growth area in publishing, yet some people regard it as an artificial and quite unnecessary category. Haven't children, in the past, managed to make the transition from *The Jungle Book* to *Animal Farm* without too much difficulty?

Admittedly the young adult novel appears to be something of a hybrid, but one reason for its growth may well be found in the current state of the adult fiction market. The young reader who is ready and eager to move on to something meatier finds that the choice lies between a few interesting but difficult "literary" novels on the one hand and a mass of genre fiction on the other. What he needs is a book that will hold his interest, widen his horizons, and deepen his understanding of human relationships, and this is exactly what the best of young adult fiction sets out to do.

Who are these "young adults"

Once upon a time they were known as teenagers. More recently they have been termed "new adults" or, more commonly, "young adults" and are usually defined as being between 12 and 16 years of age. This, of course, is intended only as a rough marketing guide: everyone accepts that children mature at different rates and cannot possibly be so neatly classified. It is also generally agreed that they vary enormously as regards intellectual ability and background, and it is therefore only right and proper that the books provided for them should reflect this difference and cater for all their needs.

If there is a common denominator, it must surely be the profound physical and emotional upheaval that marks the transition from childhood to adulthood. Like the younger children's need to test their courage by reading ghost and horror stories, adolescents may also use books as a kind of sounding board. Reading how fictional characters cope with problems they may share, such as the agony of shyness or the difficulty of making parents realise they're no longer children, will at the very least make them feel they're not alone. At best, it may even help them find their way through the labryinth. If you were yourself a bookish child, you can probably remember that books were not only a great comfort to you at this time, but they also assumed an almost mystical significance.

It is interesting to note that Salinger's *Catcher in the Rye* and William Golding's *Lord of the Flies*, both categorised as adult novels, are enormously popular with adolescents. Surely it is not mere coincidence that these two books are about self-discovery, and the seemingly impossible task of coming to terms with the adult world?

The problems children have to face while making this transition will inevitably be determined by their particular situation and it is as well to acknowledge now that what you write is unlikely to be relevant to *every* child in *every* situation – at least, not unless it's so general as to be bland and superficial. The best guide when choosing the theme of your book must surely be to draw on your own experience as a teenager. Think back to your main preoccupations at that time and see how they can be translated into today's terms. Don't forget you'll have the advantage of being able to synthesize, making sense of what may at the time have seemed utter confusion. You can also use any expert knowledge you may have acquired along the way to enrich the background of the book, so that the situation you're dealing with can be fleshed out with interesting detail.

This means, inevitably, that you'll be looking at the situation from a subtly altered vantage point. Nonetheless, if you're writing about something that once made a deep impression on you, and are able to recreate the emotions you felt at the time, the chances are that your book will strike a chord in the mind of some receptive reader.

No concessions

At the top end of the market you will find books that make little or no concession to mass popularity. These are aimed at the highly literate child and are intended to stretch and challenge the intellect. For this reason they may appeal equally to the discriminating adult, which is why most enlightened libraries stock such books both in the children's section and on the adult fiction shelves. Some, like Robert Cormier's *I am the Cheese*, use the kind of complex narrative technique more usually found in an adult novel. Others, like Alan Garner's *The Owl Service*, demand a high level of emotional understanding.

Clearly these are not quite children's books; yet they are not quite adult books either. In *The Signal Approach to Children's Books* Jill Paton Walsh is quoted as saying that if she'd intended to write *Goldengrove* or *Unleaving* for adults, she would have approached the writing quite differently. The distinction is a fine one, and has little to do with the relative difficulty of language or ideas. The ability to pitch the tone of a book towards a specific readership is, I suspect, largely a matter of instinct; but finding the level at which you, the writer, are able to say what you want to say, without any sense of constraint or limitation, is vital to the success of your book.

Complexity of ideas, of course, doesn't necessarily demand complexity of language. The best writers in this field have mastered the art of expressing themselves in clear, direct prose refreshingly free of literary mannerisms. In *Unleaving* Jill Paton Walsh uses language with sharp, almost crystalline precision, to convey great intensity of feeling. This is how she describes Madge's return to a small Cornish town after some years' absence, arriving by train very early in the morning:

> Madge has been all night without sleep; she is light-headed. She feels as insubstantial as the town, mistily present, hovering vaguely in the gentle dawn. The sea in the harbour is shallow, creeping softly, with little waves breaking at the last moment, in small hushed splashings, as though not to wake, as though to come tiptoe up to the leaning boats, and quiet dew-sleeked quays. What do I feel? Madge thinks. Do I feel anything? I have come, that is all.

The wonderfully liberating message for the writer is, therefore, Don't be afraid to set sail on difficult waters. Provided your vessel is seaworthy and you are prepared to trim your sails when necessary, there's really nothing to stop you going wherever you want to go.

The need for honesty

The range of books written today for the young adult market is considerable – rightly so, since not all adolescents will find what they're looking for among the novels that receive the highest critical acclaim. There are different kinds of intelligence as well as different levels of attainment; and publishers have been quick to recognise the need for books that are accessible to a wide variety of readers.

The American writer, Paul Zindel, is immensely popular with young adults. This may be partly due to his style – light and entertaining, with never a hint of pomposity – and partly to the way he manages to combine realism with humour and toughness with compassion. In *The Pigman* he tells the story of a 14-year-old girl and a 15-year-old boy's involvement with a lonely old man, Mr Pignati, who desperately needs company. Their relationship with him is balanced precariously between farce and tragedy, giving the book a quality of nervous tension that puts it in a class above mere entertainment.

Honesty is an essential ingredient in the good young adult novel. In Lynn Reid Banks' *My Darling Villain*, set against a contemporary background, there is a superb description of a teenage party that goes badly wrong after the arrival of some gatecrashers.

(Tina) looked at me, this sort of zany grin still on her face, and then started to come back to herself. She went all white and started to sway, her mouth open. "Gosh, Kate – I'm sorry –" she gasped, and then said in quite a different voice. "I'm going to throw up."

"In the loo," I said, and pushed her through into the hall cloakroom. Then I rushed back. There was a lull. The bread-fighters were standing around, panting and half-laughing and looking sort of dazed and silly. Ian was leaning against the wall with his eyes closed. Claudia lifted her hand to throw the last soggy bit of punch-fruit at Moti, but I had lost all my inhibitions by this time and just knocked it out of her fingers.

"Pigs!" I burst out. "You're pigs, all of you! Look at the carpet – look at the table – look at yourselves! You're no better than –" But I couldn't think of anything bad enough.

This is a world the young adult reader will instantly recognise. It's real, it's true: the problems that face Kate, who is telling the story, are the kind of problems that most of them will at some time have encountered.

It's at this stage that a divergence seems to occur in the literary tastes of boys and girls, a fact which is sometimes blamed on to sexist stereotyping. A far more likely reason is that their physical and emotional responses to the onset of puberty are quite different. Whereas most boys like to imagine how they would cope with the kind of challenge to be found in the realms of fantasy, space fiction, and thrillers, girls are more concerned about their ability to handle relationships. This is not to say that boys *never* read young adult fiction: that would be far too sweeping a generalisation and demonstrably untrue, since many books can be enjoyed equally by both sexes. Most writers, however, are prepared to recognise this difference without necessarily exploiting it.

Stereotyping, sexist or otherwise, should of course be strenuously avoided. It is undoubtedly a form of laziness, implying that you prefer to follow a hackneyed formula rather than take a fresh look at the world about you. Babette Cole's *Princess Smartypants* makes us chuckle because it turns the old fairy-tale upside down and gives the traditional happy ending a real sting in the tail. On the other hand, there's no need to go over the top: not all Mums are nuclear physicists and not all Dads wear aprons and do the housework. As long as you bear in mind that times have changed and stereotypes are boring, you should get the balance about right.

Publishers are constantly on the look-out for books that deal realistically with the world we live in today. They would love to receive more manuscripts from writers who have first-hand experience of growing up in a multi-racial society, especially those from ethnic minorities. Bear in mind, though, the advice given by Beverley Anderson in the Good Book Guide to Children's Books:

> What matters is that "multicultural" books should be as interesting and well-written as any others and that they can be enjoyed by the children who come from the communities they describe without embarrassment, anxiety, or irritation. A feebly plotted, clumsily written book by someone from the appropriate background is no more acceptable than a similar book by an outsider.

Two books she particularly recommends are Anita Desai's *The*

Village by the Sea and Farrukh Dhondy's *Come to Mecca*.

Any theme, from politics to sexual and social problems, is acceptable, provided it is dealt with honestly and with sensitivity. Be warned, though, of the danger of trying to "manufacture" a book. It is unwise to take a cool, calculated look at the market, decide that publishers are going for inner-city novels at the moment, and set about trying to write one, without ever having lived in an inner city yourself. The result will almost certainly be unconvincing, peopled by the kind of "stock" characters you imagine may live in tower blocks but who in fact are little more than caricatures. You can only write truthfully about what you know; and if your own experience seems to you not only limited but irrelevant, remember that not all children live in inner cities; and even those that do may enjoy reading about somewhere different for a change. It is far more important to get the emotional content of the book right, and you can only do that by writing from the heart. So put honesty first: it's by far the best policy.

The teenage romance

If you look along the shelves of your local bookshop you will find a mass of popular fiction aimed specifically at girls. There has in recent years been a boom in the publication of teenage romances, mainly original paperbacks, and at present they appear to be still gaining in popularity.

Is this necessarily a bad thing?

There are two points to bear in mind. The first is that many teenagers, searching for something light and easy to read, can quickly become addicted to the kind of pulp romantic fiction intended for the adult market, which is mainly glossy, unrealistic, and often verging on "soft porn". The second is that not all teenage romances can be lumped together: there's a vast difference between them, a fact which is sometimes obscured by unimaginative packaging. The jackets, presumably designed to catch the eye of a browsing teenager, are not always an accurate guide to what lies between the covers.

If you take a closer look you will find that the contents range from quite realistic – and not always romantic – stories to the kind of junior historical romp known in the trade as "liberty bodice rippers". Some are blatantly escapist; others attempt to offer something better than the young reader will find in an adult romance, namely deeper characterisation and a more honest approach to human relationships.

In Anthea Cohen's novel *Substance and Shadow* the central character, Jenny, is a student nurse. When she enters the clinic room to see Staff Nurse Maxwell slipping a handful of disposable syringes into her uniform pocket, she is presented with a more difficult situation than she's ever had to cope with before.

> When I get to the changing room it's empty, there's no one to have a natter with. Perhaps if one of my mates had been there it wouldn't have hit me, about Maxwell I mean, but it does. I suddenly feel I *must* tell Sister Holt about Staff Maxwell and the syringes – I have to – this isn't school where you mustn't snitch on anyone you see doing something wrong, something that really doesn't affect anyone else though like having a quick drag behind the bicycle shed or stealing notebooks and pens out of the stationery cupboard when it's found unlocked. This is different, this is grown-up stuff, dangerous.

Here Anthea Cohen is writing from her own nursing experience, and the problems that Jenny has to cope with are very different from those that occupy the heroine of a traditional escapist romance.

The difficulties experienced by children of broken homes is a fairly common theme, but it doesn't have to be given a downbeat treatment. In my own book *The French Summer* 15-year-old Emma and her younger brother Daniel belong to a single-parent family, but their real problems arise whenever their somewhat erratic mother Keeley toys with the idea of getting married again.

> "Blossoms, I've just met the most interesting man," she would tell us, all starry-eyed. "I just *know* you're going to like him."
>
> And on the whole we did like them, sometimes a lot. But it didn't make any difference, because they were always the same type – itinerant artists, out-of-work musicians, roving TV reporters. In other words, they weren't natural providers, any more than our father was a natural provider. And the prospect of being saddled with a couple of healthy, growing kids frightened them away, just as it had frightened our father away. Keeley on her own they would have settled for, gladly; but Daniel and I were a terrible handicap. The trouble was that she could never accept this, so it would all end in tears and we'd have to pick up the pieces and carry on as before, until the next time.

And when Keeley eventually does find a natural provider, a charming but staid Frenchman who invites them to spend a month in Brittany getting to know his own family, the outcome is by no means a neatly contrived "happy ending".

There are, of course, guidelines laid down for the authors of these books. The tone may be tender, funny, down-to-earth, but not sentimental, moralistic, or graphically sexual. The style, while colloquial, should not include profanity, obscenity, or a heavy use of dialect or slang. You are therefore subject to certain limitations and if you think this would cramp your style then you'd be wise not to try.

If, however, you feel you'd like to find out more about the teenage romance market, why not write off to a few publishers asking them to send you a copy of their guidelines? They are usually only too happy to give you information, being constantly on the search for new writers.

Fashions and fads

Whenever I talk to a group of people about writing for young adults the question always arises, "How can one be sure of being up-to-date when teenage fashions change so rapidly?"

The answer is that you can't. That's why it is advisable to avoid being too specific, such as referring to pop records, current crazes, or even words and phrases that may be in vogue now but will be old hat by the time your book is published. If you want to mention a rock star make sure it's someone whose appeal is likely to last a very long time. It is essential that your dialogue should sound young, natural, and lively, but you can achieve this without the use of too much current slang.

It is best not to try too hard to be trendy. Teenage culture, fed by specialist magazines which are by their very nature ephemeral, is inevitably something of a closed book to most adults. Your novel, you hope, will have a far longer shelf life. This doesn't mean, of course, that you needn't do any research. You can learn a great deal by watching and listening to teenagers, as well as reading their magazines and watching television programmes intended specifically for them.

When it comes to clothes, the continuing appeal of jeans for both sexes is a great blessing for writers; and if the situation calls for something more unusual you can always use a little ingenuity. In my updated fairy-tale *Cinderella in Blue Jeans* I solved the ball-gown problem by having my heroine hire a genuine 'thirties evening dress for one night only; this not only fitted in well with the plot but also enabled me to describe a dress that was already so far out-of-date that it had become timeless.

In fact it's amazing how little some things change. If you visit a disco you'll find that, apart from obvious technical innovations, the ritual taking place on the dance floor is as old as the hills. My advice, therefore, is not to worry too much about current fads and fashions. Write the book you want to write and check out the details later. You may be pleasantly surprised how little you have to alter.

One way of avoiding the issue altogether is to set your story back in time. The placing of Mary Melford's novel *The Watcher Bee* against the background of a Midland farming community in the 'twenties and 'thirties, is what gives the book its wonderfully haunting, atmospheric quality. Nonetheless many teenagers of today can easily identify with Kate, the "watcher bee" of the title, who wonders if she is destined forever to be one of life's onlookers. And in one of the most popular series ever written for young adults, K.M. Peyton's four Flambards books, Christina is shown growing up against a background of the birth of aviation and the First World War. Surely this disproves yet again the fallacious idea that teenagers only want to read books that mirror their own lives and are set in their own time.

How frank can you be?

No-one who has read a newspaper recently can fail to be aware of the kind of pressures many teenagers are subjected to. Parental abuse, drugs, AIDS, and the dangers of casual sex are all discussed openly in schools and on television. Surely, therefore, the fiction provided for this age group should also deal fully and frankly with these matters?

Some of it does. It entirely depends on the policy of the publishing house concerned. Many are prepared to consider – and may indeed welcome – a book that pulls no punches either in content or in the language it uses. Judy Blume, whose books are extremely popular with young readers, never flinches from presenting the more basic aspects of life. Her book *Forever* deals frankly with teenage sex; *Are You There, God? It's me, Margaret* describes a young girl's first experience of menstruation.

It must be said, however, that the recent crop of novels about specific sexual/social problems are not on the whole remarkable for their literary merit. Again, most of them have the unmistakable stamp of a "manufactured" book.

At the other end of the scale, many publishers of teenage romances will consider only material that is (by their definition) "squeaky clean". They don't want explicit sex, nor will they allow profane or obscene language. Sex can be mentioned, of course, as long as the emphasis is on the emotional aspect rather than the physical. Drug abuse is not an acceptable subject for this genre; nor is any kind of sexual abuse.

You will, therefore, have to do your market research in order to find the publishers who are most likely to be sympathetic to your own approach. Generally speaking, though, it is not so much a matter of what you say as the way you say it. Pretty well any subject is okay provided it is treated with sensitivity and an awareness of your potential readership. Young adults, however tough they may appear to be on the outside, are at an emotionally vulnerable age. To offer them problems without the hope of finding a solution would be irresponsible. Be as frank as you want to be; but there should always be – in my opinion, at least – a glimmer of light at the end of the tunnel.

A comment given to me by John Escott, author of several books for young adults, puts the whole question into perspective. "I don't think of the people I write for as belonging to any particular age group," he said. "I just assume that what offends me will probably also offend them. So really there's no problem."

8

FANTASY AND SCIENCE FICTION

Make-believe is not merely a game to a child, it's a serious business. Watch any group of children at play and they will almost certainly be acting out a fantasy, with as many rules and regulations as any adult society can dream up. Like tiger cubs pouncing on an imaginary prey, they are preparing for life.

Diana Wynne Jones, writing in the quarterly magazine *Books for Your Children* in 1981, says: "It does seem that a fantasy, working out in its own terms, stretching you beyond the normal concerns of your own life, gains you a peculiar charge of energy which inexplicably enriches you. At least, this is my ideal of a fantasy, and I am always trying to write it."

Fantasy is by its very nature almost impossible to define. It can be humorous and cosy; or it can be on an epic, mythological scale. It can have its roots in our familiar, everyday world; or it can be about other worlds and other times. It is sometimes allied to science fiction, as in this chapter; and in recent years it has gained a quite remarkable hold on the popular imagination through the introduction of fighting games such as Dungeons and Dragons.

For the writer it offers an enormously rich field of possibility. We are into the realms of "What if . . .?" which means that there are virtually no restraints on your creativity. Anything goes – provided, of course, that you make it credible. Your story must be entirely convincing, otherwise your readers won't be able to achieve that "willing suspension of disbelief" so essential to their enjoyment.

The invasion of magic

Some writers take normality as their starting point, placing children in a recognisably real setting before they introduce the fantastical element. P.L. Travers' *Mary Poppins* is a good example – it is worth reading the original book if you've only seen the film – and so is E. Nesbitt's *Five Children and It*, in which the Psammead, a Sand Fairy, appears with the power to grant wishes. The attraction of this kind of story is that young readers can easily imagine themselves in a similar situation. How interesting life would be if the old rug on the living-room floor were to become a magic carpet; or if an unpopular teacher turned out to be a witch in disguise.

Another bonus is the opportunity this offers for humour. You have only to introduce one unlikely factor to open up a whole new area of comic possibility. Roald Dahl is a writer who has explored this field to great effect. In *James and the Giant Peach*, from the moment James escapes from his unpleasant aunts through a tunnel leading to the centre of an enormous peach, the story takes off into the realms of wild and often hilarious imagination.

The magic may also appear in another guise, as a more ancient form of enchantment. In John Masefield's *Box of Delights*, which has recently – thanks to the television series – found a new generation of readers, Kay Harker's adventures begin when he meets the strange Punch and Judy man who entrusts him with the magic Box of Delights. By means of the box, Kay visits the past and meets such charismatic characters as The White Lady and Herne the Hunter. Brilliant though the television adaptation was, however, it didn't – for me, at least, – quite have the magic of the earlier radio version, which perhaps suggests that fantastical images are best left to the imagination. This is one of the areas where books – and radio – undoubtedly score over television.

Herne the Hunter figures also in Susan Cooper's *The Dark is Rising*, in which the eternal conflict of good and evil is fought out against a background of everyday life in the Buckinghamshire countryside. At this level magic is treated not as a springboard for humour but as a potent and mysterious force.

As you can see, the scope is limitless. All you need is to find a fresh approach, bearing in mind that friendly dragons, witches-in-disguise, and bumbling giants have been rather overworked. But if you take the invasion of magic as your starting point, it isn't hard to imagine the kind of havoc that can follow even in this material age – perhaps *especially* in this material age. And if it leads to enlightenment as well, then you'll have produced a satisfying book.

Through the looking glass

Alice falling down the rabbit-hole to find herself in a world that rapidly became curiouser and curiouser was undoubtedly the point when fantasy fiction really took off. By taking a child out of her familiar setting and placing her in a totally unfamiliar one, Lewis Carroll hit on an idea that has been fascinating writers – and readers – ever since.

The method of transition from reality to fantasy is a good test of a writer's ingenuity. The four children in C.S. Lewis's *The Lion, the Witch and the Wardrobe* discover Narnia by accident when one of them hides in a wardrobe. In Alan Garner's *Elidor* the four children find their way into the kingdom of Elidor through an old church on a demolition site in Manchester. In each case the method of transition helps to set the pattern, as when Alice stepped through the looking glass to find herself in a mirror world. What happens next will almost certainly reflect the main preoccupations of you, the writer.

It is interesting that both C.S. Lewis and Alan Garner chose to build their stories around the contrasting characters of *four* children. Whether or not this was a conscious use of Jung's concept of the quaternity, there is no doubt that fantasy fiction lends itself to interpretation on more than one level. *The Lion, the Witch and the Wardrobe* contains some obvious Christian allegory; and Alan Garner is always very much concerned with the conflict between good and evil. This may be why, as a genre, it appeals particularly to the more serious writer. Sending a fictional character on a quest, and making him encounter all kinds of adventures in an alien and often illogical world, is an accepted device for exploring the unconscious.

The introduction of symbolism for its own sake, though, can be dangerous. It is one thing to build your story on a sound mythological structure – most writers do this all the time, whether consciously or unconsciously – but quite another to let the myth take over at the expense of credibility. If you base your characters on archetypes, no matter how powerful and significant, they will inevitably appear as stereotypes. They must be free to breathe and act as they wish, not restricted by being made to fit into a strict mythological pattern.

As for the use of dreams – well, it was all right for Lewis Carroll to make Alice escape by waking up, since he was probably the first to think of it. But if you end a story now with the words, "After all, it was only a dream!" your reader will close the book with a deep and heartfelt groan of disappointment.

Experiments with time

If you've ever stood on the ramparts of Carisbrooke Castle, or in the shadows of Stonehenge, and wished you could be transported back in time, you'll be aware of the story possibilities that lie in exploring the fourth dimension.

Lucy M. Boston's writing career began when she went to live at Green Knowe. She discovered that within the Georgian framework of her new home lay the remains of a much older house, and in uncovering the original masonry she found the inspiration to write a whole series of novels. In the first of these, *The Children of Green Knowe*, Tolly comes to stay at the house with his great-aunt and meets and plays with children who have been dead for centuries. Strictly speaking, it's a ghost story; but it is the impact of the past on the present that makes the strongest impression on the reader.

This impact is also evident in the work of Penelope Lively. Set firmly in a contemporary landscape of motorways and supermarkets, her books are mainly concerned with the continuity of life. Our past is also our present: we cannot separate the two. Her first novel, *Astercote*, tells of a Cotswold village where the population was, in medieval times, virtually wiped out by the Black Death, and even today is held in the grip of superstition. If there is an element of fantasy here it's largely in the mind; but none the less powerful for that.

Most children have a strong sense of history, although it's worth remembering, when writing for the very young, that the actual time scale doesn't mean a great deal. 1066 and 1812 are much the same as far as a 7-year-old is concerned. Prehistory, though, has an endless fascination for them, and they can make the imaginative time-leap from the present day to the Stone Age with no difficulty at all. A favourite book is Clive King's *Stig of the Dump*, in which Barney finds Stig, a left-over caveman, living in a rubbish dump. The story is set in the present, but on midsummer night Barney sees Stig's Stone Age encampment on the Sussex Downs.

The possibility of a character slipping out of his own time into another has proved a fruitful source of inspiration for writers. One of the best examples is Penelope Farmer's *Charlotte*

Sometimes, in which Charlotte changes places with a ghost of her own age and goes back in time. Eventually she becomes confused: is she really Charlotte or is she Clare? The story is about identity; as with Penelope Lively's books, the fantasy element is used as a means of exploring the mind.

There are, of course, no rules that say you must set your story in the present before travelling into the past. In *The Wolves of Willoughby Chase* that wonderfully inventive writer Joan Aiken has created her own historical period, the totally imaginary reign of James III. This sets her free from that perennial problem of time travellers, the inability to change the course of history.

Just one word of warning: publishers have been heard to grumble recently about the large number of timeshift stories landing on their desks, so before you send your hero back to King Arthur's court to meet Merlin, think hard – is this really an original idea?

(Answer: No, it isn't. Mark Twain thought of it first.)

Other worlds

Going one step further, you may prefer to leave the real world behind altogether and take your readers into new and uncharted territory. Here you are totally in command: you can create new planets, new societies, new religions. Before letting all this power go to your head, however, it is as well to bear in mind that, however strange your imaginary world may be, your readers will need something they can recognise, some points of reference they can hang on to. Otherwise they'll be lost.

Tove Jansson's Moominland is unmistakeably her native Finnish landscape, inhabited by strange little creatures which look something like baby hippopotamuses. In *Finn Family Moomintroll* the Moomins hibernate in the long winter; they have adventures but can always go home to the comforting presence of Moominmamma. In other words, the Moomins are really children-in-disguise, enjoying far more freedom than their human counterparts, but living within the reassuring structure of family life.

The popularity of J.R.R. Tolkien's *The Lord of the Rings* is now legendary, but for younger children *The Hobbit* may have a more immediate appeal. Bilbo Baggins, like Don Quixote, is a comic figure who becomes a hero in spite of himself. His quest for treasure is told in terms of high adventure, but can also be interpreted as a journey of self-discovery. The child who enjoys *The Hobbit* will almost certainly move on to books conceived and written on the epic scale.

It is generally accepted that epic fantasy appeals to a very particular kind of child: one who may or may not be academically gifted, but who has sufficient powers of concentration to enter another world and remain there for long stretches of time. Often he isn't at all attracted by other kinds of fiction and will turn to non-fiction for the rest of his reading. If you were yourself this kind of child, the chances are you may find this to be your natural *métier*. If not, be careful how you tread. The *aficionados* of this genre tend to be highly critical.

At its best, epic fantasy makes strong demands on the intellectual capabilities of a young reader. It deals in allegory, philosophy, politics, and poetry; and in creating new worlds, often complicated and detailed in structure, it offers agile, fast-developing young minds the kind of nourishment they need. Interestingly, these new worlds – especially those that are post-holocaust – often bear a striking resemblance to primitive societies of the past, so that life in the 21st century seems strangely akin to life in the Dark Ages. Perhaps this is why the child who enjoys historical fiction may be equally drawn to the genre of epic fantasy.

For the writer, however, there are certain pitfalls to be avoided. It is all too easy to create a hero who is little more than a comic strip character, uniformly brave and noble, with no interesting quirks or weaknesses to make him memorable. And in trying to achieve a grandeur of style to match the epic theme, you may well end up using stilted, pompous prose, curiously lacking in humour.

These are not criticisms that can be levelled against Jan Mark. In *Divide and Rule* her central character Hanno has been chosen as the Ritual Shepherd, which means that he is forced against his will to give a year of his life to the service of the temple. Here Dow, one of the Temple Guardians is showing him around.

"This is the Hall of the Guardians," said Dow. "And that door, there, leads to the Hall of the Handmaidens. In here, the Hall of the Mechanicals –"

"The whats?"

"Mechanicals. The masons, gardeners, launderers, dairymen, cooks. You may never pass through any of these doors. This is the cookhouse, where you may go, but I won't take you in there now. They'll be preparing the evening meal, and you won't be able to eat it."

"I would," said Hanno.

"I mean, you will not be allowed to eat. Or sleep," he added casually. "Tonight you must Fast and Pray."

"How often must I fast and pray?"

"One hopes that the Shepherd will Pray continually," said Dow. "But you won't have to fast again until you leave us, unless you Transgress in the meantime. But you won't be leaving us for a long time," he added, encouragingly. "Although then, I'm afraid, you have to Fast for a week."

Hanno did not pursue this depressing information. He had enough to occupy him right now.

Here the didactic utterances of Dow are given emphasis by the use of capital letters. The author's sureness of touch makes Hanno's world seem as familiar as our own, and it is this illusion of normality that makes the final outcome all the more disturbing.

Where, then, does a fantasy take place? On our own planet, at another time? In other galaxies, at other times, in societies running parallel with our own? In fact the setting is immaterial: what fantasy fiction offers to the writer is a chance to deal with subjects that may seem too vast or deep or mysterious to be dealt with any other way.

Science fiction

Where do you draw the line between fantasy and science fiction?

The word "science" implies knowledge that is proven; taken in conjunction with the word "fiction", it suggests a kind of conjectural literature, starting with known facts about the world we live in and using them as a basis for prophecy. Science fiction, then, is primarily about the future as the writer imagines it will be. If it takes a trip into the past it is only by means of a future invention, such as H.G. Wells's time machine or Dr Who's Tardis.

Imagining the future of our own civilisation has been a major preoccupation of writers from Jules Verne onwards. John Christopher, in *The Guardians*, sees England as divided into two separate societies, the Conurb and the County. On the face of it the people living in the highly populated Conurb seem happy enough, kept provided with bread and circuses; and so do the inhabitants of the County, with their stately homes, feudal system, and wide open spaces. It isn't until Rob Randall tries crossing from one to the other that he discovers how both societies are being manipulated by their rulers, the Guardians.

It is when science fiction ventures into space that the writer may, when writing specifically for children, come up against certain difficulties. The chief stumbling block is character-isation, since, if you are going for credibility, your astronauts will be adults. This is perfectly acceptable – after all, there are no children aboard the starship Enterprise – but you do have to be on your guard against portraying them as immature, overgrown kids. It is all too easy to end up with a kind of Famous Five in Space. Another difficulty is presented by the hardware: if you want to make your spacecraft believable then you must obviously be familiar with the kind of jargon that will give it that touch of authenticity. The child who enjoys space fiction will be fairly knowledgeable on the subject, so it is no use being vague and hoping for the best.

The zany adventures of *Dr Who* are ever-popular with younger children, who have a seemingly insatiable appetite for stories about space monsters, mutants, and aliens. It is an area which could well prove fruitful for the imaginative writer, since there seems to be far less space fiction produced for 8-10 year olds than for older children, yet it is the kind of story most often requested.

The older reader of science fiction may well find his tastes already catered for by writers of the calibre of Arthur C. Clarke, Frederick Pohl, John Wyndham, and Brian Aldiss. Robert A. Heinlen's refreshingly unstuffy approach goes down particularly well with young adults and he is a master of his craft. In *Between Planets* he tells the story of Don Harvey, chosen to carry an important message from Earth to Mars, who ends up on Venus instead and finds himself in the middle of a war. Here the hardware is never allowed to get in the way of the plot.

If you have a strong desire to write this genre of fiction, the chances are that you are already a devotee of SF, in which case you won't need me to tell you the wide variety of story ideas and treatment available to you. However, it is worth bearing in mind that, despite the scientific trappings, space fiction works best when it is based firmly in the mainstream of children's narrative literature. While making use of the ever-popular elements of adventure, horror, fantasy, and myth, the successful writer is the one who sets out primarily to tell a thumping good story.

9

NON-FICTION

Non-fiction is a convenient umbrella under which to group everything that can't be described as "a story". In a children's library it brings together such unlikely bedfellows as History, Sport, Nature, Biography, Religion, Science, Jokes, and even Poetry. It can cover complex subjects very briefly, as in an encyclopaedia, and quite simple subjects at length, as in an information book. For the writer it offers a wonderful opportunity to work in his own special field of interest, and to share that interest with a wide and receptive readership.

Children love to collect facts and store them, either in their memories or in notebooks. Ask any child about his favourite subject and you'll probably be amazed at the extent of his knowledge; and it may well be a subject that continues to absorb him for several years, even a lifetime. This is one of the reasons why a non-fiction book tends to have a longer shelf life than a novel. It may not make its author a literary celebrity or earn him a fabulous advance against royalties, but it can establish his reputation with publishers and continue to bring in a steady flow of royalties long after his novels have been forgotten.

The quality of non-fiction books for children has improved beyond recognition during the last 20 years. In the past most factual books were frankly dull, as well as being limited as regards subject matter. Nowadays there is a wide variety of material available on almost every subject you can think of; and most of it is imaginatively written, well-produced, and lavishly illustrated.

Almost every subject – therein lies the problem as far as the writer is concerned; namely, how to find either a new subject or a new slant on an old subject. So where do you begin?

Starting points

Geoffrey Lamb, who has written or edited about 25 educational books for Harrap, says: "My first published book was a prose anthology for use in schools. I had seen a prose anthology about Children in Literature on the shelves of a local library, and after glancing through it I thought (rather contemptuously) that any fool could do a book like that. Then the thought struck me I ought to try one myself! Eventually, after a good many tries with a good many publishers, Harrap accepted my scheme."

Like Geoffrey Lamb, many educational writers started out as teachers: some, indeed, continue to combine both careers. Textbooks, especially, tend to be written by people actively involved in education, who have studied their subject in depth and know what is required in a classroom situation.

The vast majority of non-fiction books for children, however, are not designed as teachers' instructional aids, but as sources of background knowledge for the child to use by himself. As every teacher knows, there's nothing a child likes better than to be given a project book and told he can write about any subject he chooses. Even a reluctant reader will spend hours poring over information books that may help him to discover what he needs to know. With the current emphasis on encouraging children to gather and record information from various sources, educational publishers will be looking out for good new material.

If you are a teacher yourself, you may already have an idea of what is needed. How often have you searched for a book to help you with a particular lesson and found that there isn't one that gives you exactly what you want? Fiona Reynoldson, who writes educational books on her own subject, history, offers this advice: "If you see a gap in the market either approach a sales representative who may be visiting your school, or write to a publisher you respect with an outline of your idea and perhaps a sample chapter. If they like it they will probably ask for a couple of chapters and a synopsis before discussing a possible contract. Be prepared to explain where your book fits into the market."

You may not, however, be a teacher. You may be a parent, a computer analyst, or a birdwatcher – and quite possibly all three. Whichever you are, you can make good use of your knowledge and experience, since the best starting point – as always – is to write about what you know. It is not a good idea to select a subject which has only mildly interested you in the past and to try to produce a book by doing copious research. The chances are that you will simply regurgitate other people's words and the result will be stilted and lacklustre. If, on the other hand, you choose a subject that is dear to your heart, you'll be able to communicate your enthusiasm and interest to your readers.

Subject matter

You may find it useful to make a list of possible topics and then try looking at them from several different angles. What you need to find is a new approach, and preferably one that concentrates on a single aspect of the subject. Too general a treatment will inevitably be superficial.

Take sport. Clearly, you'd have to narrow that down to one particular activity. If you chose tennis, there'd be several options open to you: you could, for example, take the history of the game; or you could write short biographical studies, with photographs, of the present-day international stars; or narrow that down even further to concentrate on one particularly distinguished player, such as Martina Navratilova. To write an instructional book on how to play the game you obviously need to have had coaching experience, in which case you should attach details of your qualifications when first submitting your idea to a publisher.

Information books can be about anything from dinosaurs to computers, but clearly it is best to avoid those areas which have been well and truly covered already. If you can be forward-looking in your choice, so much the better. The recent upsurge of interest in healthy living is reflected in the Franklin Watts series *Life Guides*, in which the medical writer Brian Ward has written four books, dealing with Diet, First Aid, Dental Care, and Exercise. In *Diet and Nutrition* he takes a close look at such subjects as additives, ethnic eating, energy, and obesity. Another recent series is *Dataworld*, produced by Grafton Books, in which the author Robin Kerrod explains how today's hi-tech communications systems work. The topics he covers in *Sound and Vision* include digital discs, cable and satellite TV, and viewdata, all of which will be of absorbing interest to today's technologically-minded child.

Nor have the arts been neglected. *Visiting an Exhibition* takes children on a light-hearted trip around museums and art galleries, combining full-colour reproductions of paintings and artefacts with lively comments from the cartoon-character onlookers. Laurene Krasny Brown, who is co-author of the book with Marc Brown, says, "We saw there was a need for a book that prepares young children for visiting art museums and introduces them to the appreciation of art. We created this book to fill that gap."

This brings us back to the importance of finding the gaps. What you are looking for is a topic which, in your opinion, is crying out to have a book written about it. As soon as you have the germ of an idea you should investigate thoroughly the non-fiction shelves of your public or school library, as well as those of your local bookseller, to check that there really is a gap in the market. Even if there is already a book dealing with your topic, you may be able to find a slightly different approach that will enable you to bring in fresh material. When you have a clear picture of what's needed, you are ready to start planning your book.

Research

Having decided on your topic, you come to what is in my opinion the most enjoyable part – the acquisition of material. It is unlikely, as well as undesirable, that you'll be able to do this entirely by reading books: depending on your subject, of course, some kind of practical research will almost certainly have to be undertaken. This may entail visits to factories, museums, public record offices, or even, for the writer of geographical subjects, other countries – all tax deductable, of course!

Gwynneth Ashby, writer of many junior travel books, warns that the research can take as long as the writing of the book. Her last book *Korean Village* was only 2,000 words in length, but the research in South Korea took four months. She also stresses that, however thorough you are, there is always a danger of small inaccuracies creeping in, which is why she takes the precaution of sending her text to be checked by a national of the country before allowing it to go to print.

Generally speaking, experts in any field are only too happy to give you information: Indeed, there's nothing they like better than being asked to talk about their favourite subject. The resources of your local reference library are also there to be tapped; and the librarian will, on request, prepare a bibliography of books available so that you can choose which ones you'd like them to obtain. One reference book you'll find invaluable is Ann Hoffmann's *Research for Writers*, which will answer any questions you may have on where to go for information.

It is advisable to double-check any facts you may acquire from books, since it is not unknown for one writer to make a mistake which is then passed on to every other writer who uses his work as a source of material. Accuracy is vital. You should never underestimate a young reader's ability to spot any weak areas in your knowledge. Children are highly critical of mistakes and will soon lose faith in a book if they suspect that its author isn't master of his subject.

It is as well to bear in mind, too, that your book may be used in countries other than your own, which means that any examples or comparisons you make should be as international as possible. You should also avoid giving too many statistics, or referring to current rates of exchange, since these can so quickly become inaccurate. This is a constant hazard for the non-fiction writer; if his book is reprinted he may have to rewrite whole chapters in order to bring his information up-to-date. Even the photographs have to be checked, in case they show buildings that no longer exist, or fail to show a skyscraper where a skyscraper now stands.

Concept and structure

Having done your research, you should ask yourself the question, What sort of a book is it going to be? Instructional? Scholarly? Entertaining? The answer may well be a combination of all three, but you need to have it quite clear in your mind before you are ready to start work.

Clearly your overall concept will be determined by the way in which you intend the book to be used. If it is designed primarily as an aid for the teacher, then you must take into account the need for flexibility. All teachers teach differently according to their personalities, and may be working anywhere from an inner city area in Sheffield to a small farming community in the Outer Hebrides. Fiona Reynoldson says she includes plenty of exercises that can be used by hard-pressed teachers if they wish, but warns against suggesting additional work such as building a medieval fort in the playground. Teachers can think up that sort of exercise for themselves!

If, on the other hand, your book is intended for young children to use on their own, or possibly for the older but less able child, you will need to structure it accordingly. Write simply and in short sentences. Break up your text with subheadings to make it easier for them to grasp the essential facts. If you suggest things to do, make sure they don't involve the use of materials that are difficult to get hold of, or that might be dangerous for children working on their own.

When writing for any age group it is important that the text should be clear and informative, so that a child can absorb the information easily, even if the subject matter is difficult. Many educational writers find it helps to build the book around a specific child with whom readers can identify – bearing in mind, of course, the need to maintain a balance between the sexes. If you choose a girl as your central character, you must also show the life of her male counterpart (perhaps her brother?), and try to feature both equally in the illustrations.

Margery Fisher, in her appraisal of non-fiction for children, *Matters of Fact*, says that an information book should contain fact, concept, and attitude. In other words, it is just as important for the author to find the right tone of voice when writing non-fiction as it is for fiction. However hungry children may be for the information you can give them, they will soon lose their appetites if it is served up in a flat, colourless way, full of generalisations. Don't be afraid to stamp your own personality on your work. Your enthusiasm for your subject should shine through, enlivening every statement you make. Children are far more likely to warm to a book they feel has been written by a real, live person, not by a teaching machine.

When it comes to organising your material, the key word is "selection". You may, in the end, be able to use only a fraction of your research; but there is no virtue in cramming a book with facts for their own sake. Deciding what to leave out is just as important as deciding what to put in; and once you have discarded everything that is irrelevant to your theme, you'll be ready to start knocking what's left into some of sort of shape. It may take time and a great deal of trouble to get it right. Be prepared to make changes at every stage of your work. If you establish good relations with your local school you may be able to discuss your ideas with the Head and even test sections of your book on the children. They will soon tell you if they find the text boring or too difficult!

One final word – indexing. When children are looking for information, it is essential that they should be able to find it quickly and easily. Learning how to use an index is also good training for any studying they may do in later life.

Illustrations

All young children will choose a book with plenty of pictures in preference to one that is solid text. Illustrations bring a subject to life and, as in picture books, can work with the text to add a new dimension to a child's understanding. No matter how vivid the words you use to describe what a tiger looks like to a child who has never seen one, a picture will do the job twice as well – and in half the time.

Gwynneth Ashby says, "Illustrations in project books vary: some have line drawings in addition to colour and black-and-white photographs. If possible take your own photographs, particularly colour, making sure that you take colour slides and not prints. Excellent black-and-white glossy photographs can be obtained – usually free of charge provided acknowledgement is made – from the Foreign Ministry of the country in which you are travelling. If you have gaps, or need photographs to illustrate historical source material, consult the BALPA (British Association of Picture Libraries and Agencies) Directory, which is published annually by the British Association of Picture Libraries and Agencies, PO Box 4, Andoversford, Cheltenham, Glos."

Even if you are not a photographer yourself, you still need to consider carefully what kind of pictures would best accompany your text, since it is important that they should be there for a purpose and not as mere decoration. It may be possible for you to team up with a good photographer and work in collaboration; or, failing that, perhaps you can visit the picture libraries yourself to find exactly what you want. Once your book is accepted, of course, professional help will be available, and ideally you will be able to work in close liaison with the illustrator or researcher assigned to you. If you look at the picture acknowledgements at the back of *Discovering Squirrels*, published in Wayland's *Discovering Nature* series, you will see that credits are given to over 30 photographers. The quality of the illustrations in this series as a whole suggests that a great deal of care has been taken to find the best available.

If your subject needs to be illustrated by diagrams and you are not yourself a competent artist, don't worry: whoever is in charge of the artwork will see that your rough copy is reproduced in a professional way. It is worth bearing in mind, however, that the artist chosen by the publisher will probably have no specialised knowledge of your subject, so if accurate drawings are required to illustrate technical points you will need to draw the roughs carefully and supply a straightforward brief.

Mainly for fun

Not all non-fiction books are, strictly speaking, educational. If you have an inexhaustible supply of jokes, or if you enjoy thinking up puzzles and quizzes, you may like to explore this ever-popular corner of the market.

Another idea worth exploring is that of activity books. I have often heard parents and teachers complain about the scarcity of simple craft books, both those designed to be used by individual children at home and those intended for classroom use. Again, it is a question of looking for the gaps.

You should also bear in mind that you are writing for modern children, and the material you produce must reflect the world they live in. The biggest growth area recently has been in the field of computer books. Franklin Watts' *Micro-Fun Puzzles* are designed for use with the BBC micro-computer and include such games as an updated version of the old favourite, Hangman, in which you challenge a friend to beat the computer. And the Usborne book of *Air Travel Games* provides plenty of games, puzzles, and activities to pass away the time while held up at airports or on a long, boring flight. It can also provide vicarious enjoyment for the child who isn't able to travel anywhere by air.

The main intention of these books is to entertain, but that doesn't mean they have no educational value. Any book that demands some kind of active participation on the part of its reader will help to develop his mental agility, as well as adding to his store of general knowledge.

10

PICTURE STORIES AND ANNUALS

Often children who are not interested in reading a book will avidly devour a comic strip; and if this is deplored by parents and teachers it is worth remembering that they are absorbing words as well as pictures. Anything that encourages them to develop their reading skills must surely be a worthwhile exercise.

However, comic strips aren't only enjoyed by reluctant readers. They have a wide appeal, especially among those teenagers who wouldn't dream of reading a hardback book and regard even paperbacks with suspicion. Somehow comics have an acceptable image: and many, like *Dandy* and *Beano*, have achieved classic status.

Small wonder, then, that the picture-story industry continues to offer the writer a constant and seemingly insatiable market. What's more, you don't have to worry about finding an artist to work with, since all you are required to contribute is the script: the publisher takes care of the illustrations and the chances are that you and the artist will never meet.

What are your markets?

If you look along your local newsagent's shelves you will find that nearly all the comics available are produced by the same few publishers. One of these, Polystyle Publications Limited, which produces the magazine *Buttons* for children of *Play School* age, works mainly with regular writers connected with the TV programme on which the characters are based; so they are not really in the market for unsolicited manuscripts. However, the vast majority of weekly picture magazines are controlled by two companies: D.C. Thomson & Co Ltd. Albert Square, Dundee DD1 9QJ; and Fleetway Publications, Irwin House, 118 Southwark Street, London SE1 0SW. Both these companies are prepared to consider work from freelance writers.

Before you begin it is essential that you should study the kind of material they publish, and then tailor your story to fit the style, length, and format they require. If an editor can see you have done your homework, he's bound to be more favourably disposed towards you. Remember, he's only going to read your script once, so it is important you get it right first time.

D.C. Thomson & Co Ltd publish a range of girls' and boys' papers for readers in the 7-12 age group, as well as much longer stories in the Starblazer (science fiction) and Commando (war) Libraries. They're interested both in serials, which can be anything from four to twenty instalments, and in series of stories about the same principal character or characters. If you write to them they will send you detailed hints on picture script-writing, together with examples showing how the picture stories are interpreted by the artists from the scripts you supply.

Stories

You will get the best idea of the kind of stories wanted by studying the magazines, although D.C. Thomson warns that you shouldn't try to imitate plots already used. The publishers are looking for a wide variety of material – sport, school, science fiction, and everything else that has story value.

A picture-story is a story like any other: that is, it must have interesting characters, plenty of conflict, and be set against a believable background. It needs an arresting opening, something that will immediately catch the reader's eye and make him want to read on. It is not a good idea, for example, to start with two children going on a picnic, looking for somewhere to sit down, opening up the basket, etc. That is not nearly dramatic enough. But two children unpacking their picnic, unaware that a bull is watching them from the other end of the field . . . now that could be more promising!

I must warn you, though, that the picnic situation is something of a cliché, as are birthday parties and wanting a pet. Other situations to be avoided, because they are potentially dangerous, are children playing near water or swimming unattended, talking to strangers, or picking and eating berries.

When writing for pre-school children, you should also bear in mind that there are certain concepts they may find difficult to understand, such as "school assembly" or "secretary" or "underground train". That is not to say that these terms shouldn't be used, but it helps if you give a brief explanation.

D.C. Thomson say in their guidelines: "Writing a script is an application always of skill and thought, working out the best way of starting, the best way of development, the fullest use of atmosphere and of character and of dramatic situations."

Characters

There are two ways of approaching a publisher with a picture-script. The first is to write a story around existing characters, which means, of course, that you have to know them extremely well. The trouble is that they are probably already "spoken for" by their creator, or by one or more regular contributors who regard them as their own special property. The only practical purpose this method serves, therefore, is to demonstrate that you are capable of writing a picture-script.

The second approach is to create an entirely new character around whom you can build your story or stories. This is far more likely to catch the attention of a publisher who is looking out for fresh ideas. As with any other kind of storytelling, it is the characters who make the most impact on readers. No matter how exciting their adventures, they won't gain a devoted following unless there is something about them that readers find particularly endearing or admirable.

They may of course be animals; but if they're human they don't necessarily have to be children. There are some situations – again, science fiction offers a good example – where it would be unrealistic to have a child hero. Indeed, two of the most popular heroes of all time have been Dan Dare and, more recently, Superman. And there are scores of others.

Where your central characters are children, it is as well to make at least one of them slightly older than that of the intended readership. This is because 10-year-olds, for example, will prefer to identify with a character who is older than themselves rather than someone younger.

The format

The number of pictures or "frames" in a story can vary. A good average is about 24 frames; but longer "novels", such as the Starblazer or Commando Libraries, are of 135-145 frames.

Each frame is divided into three parts:

1 the action or "scene", described in visual terms for the artist to interpret
2 the dialogue or thoughts of the characters, shown as "balloons"
3 the narration, in the form of a caption, which can be printed

either above or below the frame

1 Of these, action is by far the most important element. Crafting a picture-story is rather like writing the scenario for a film, since the story has to unfold in terms of movement. It doesn't necessarily have to be fast or violent movement, but something must happen in each frame that will further the narrative. There is no need to record the passing of time, for example, by showing what a character is doing moment by moment. If a girl travels to visit her cousin in another country, it would be tedious to show every stage of her journey from taxi to train to boat to bus to front door to living-room. You can cover all that with a few words of dialogue as she greets her cousin: "What a journey! This is the first time I've ever been abroad." Similarly, a long sequence consisting of a static coversation between two people on a bus would have little or no story value.

Be careful you don't crowd the picture description with too much detail. For example, it wouldn't be easy for the artist to cram into one small frame several characters, a burning house, a fire engine, and firemen climbing a ladder to rescue someone from an upstairs window. When you're describing how you visualise the scene you should try to focus the action on a few dramatic essentials.

2 As in all fiction, dialogue plays a vital part in furthering the story. Since space is limited within the confines of a "balloon" the speeches must be concise and purposeful, yet appear as natural as possible.

The main points to bear in mind are:

a Each "frame" shows a single moment of time, so a character can't talk twice in the same picture

b You can't have too many people talking at once: that would be confusing in such a small space

c "Thought balloons" can be used to convey what's going

through a character's mind

If you are writing for younger children, the dialogue may be shown in the form of a narrative caption underneath the picture rather than a balloon. In this case it is as well not to open and close the quotation marks too often, since this looks messy and can be confusing. If you use reported speech now and again it will stop the caption becoming staccato.

3 A caption can:

a bring the reader up-to-date at the beginning of a serial story
b act as a narrative link, as in: "Sharon went to stay the night with her schoolfriend Lucy"
c convey the passage of time, as in: "Next morning", "Soon afterwards", or "Much later"
d set the scene, as in: "Meanwhile, back at the Simpsons' house..."

Useful as they are, however, captions should be used sparingly and kept as short as possible.

To sum up, John Escott, who writes regularly for *Buttons*, says: "'Think pictures' is the key rule. Captions and dialogue 'bubbles' reinforce what the pictures are telling the reader, especially in scripts for the very young. The best picture scripts can almost stand on their own, without words, and still tell the story."

Presentation

Your initial approach to a publisher should take the form of a brief description of the main character or characters, a story synopsis, and a sample script showing at least the first few frames. From this he will be able to tell whether or not you have a talent for this style of storytelling.

The script should be set out clearly to show:

a the caption, if required

b the scene, including all the visual elements you wish the artist to depict

c the dialogue, whether spoken or thought

Example 1:

Caption: Next day at school the twins went to see Mrs James.

Scene: Tim and Jenny confront a stern-looking Mrs James in the classroom.

Tim: We're sorry, Mrs James. We didn't mean to break the window.

Jenny: Honestly, it was an accident.

If you want to show a character on his own, thinking, the layout is as follows.

Example 2:

Scene: Close-up of Tim looking thoughtful.

Tim: I hope Mrs James doesn't find out what we were doing when we broke the window.

Photo stories

Some picture magazines for older girls, such as *Jackie*, use photographs rather than line illustrations. The scriptwriting technique is much the same, bearing in mind that the stories must be realistic and set in not-too-exotic locations. The storyline needs to be simple; and although the content is mainly romantic it should reflect life today. You don't have to supply the photographs, but you should give a rough idea of how you visualise each frame.

Again, D.C. Thomson & Co Ltd will send guidelines on request.

Annuals

Is there any market for the conventional short story, told in a straightforward narrative form?

Some magazines do include short stories, but not many. Annuals, however, will consider stories of 1000-2500 words in length, as well as picture stories of 20-60 frames.

Fame and/or fortune?

Well, if it's fame you're after, I'm afraid you'll be disappointed; all picture scriptwriters remain anonymous and aren't nearly so important as the characters they create. But, although it may be a little optimistic to speak in terms of making your fortune, regular contributors can earn a useful extra income.

If you want to build up a reputation for reliability, however, you will have to be disciplined. John Escott says: "I have one day a week when I write my weekly script and, barring a crisis or major problem, never miss. I also keep at least three scripts in hand. Not only does this give me a sense of security, it also gets me out of trouble when an additional script is asked for in a hurry, say for a special issue, as sometimes happens."

He adds a final warning: "Comics are read for fun, and if you ever lose sight of this it will show in your writing." But if you can write lively, entertaining picture stories, you are assured of a wide and faithful readership.

11

DRAMA

Every teacher knows how a sagging lesson can be miraculously revived by a touch of drama. Most children enjoy acting, especially when it involves dressing-up, and even the less confident will blossom if they can hide behind the anonymity of an actor's mask. But they also love watching plays, whether performed in the classroom or within the framework of a proscenium arch or the television screen. There is something special about drama: it fulfils a human need that goes far deeper then mere entertainment.

If you are the kind of writer who tends to think in terms of "scenes" and prefers writing dialogue to description, drama may well turn out to be your *métier*. If so, there are several options open to you, which may be summarized as follows:

1 Plays to be performed by children, usually in schools
2 Puppet plays to be performed by children
3 Plays intended to be performed by a professional theatre company
4 Radio drama for schools
5 TV drama for children

This chapter will deal with each in turn, but first we'd better take a look at the techniques of playwriting in general.

The stuff of drama

Alan Ayckbourn says:

> The whole of playwriting for me is, if you like: you get your idea, you
> get your sequence of events – which, if written literally, would take,
> say, four days at least to perform on stage – and you then have to
> select what you want your audience to see, preferably the minimum
> to allow them to understand the events.
>
> (*Conversations with Ayckbourn*, Ian Watson, pub. Macdonald
> Futura)

This is the art of the dramatist, to select and heighten the
moments that are important, and to shed those that are trivial
and boring, in order to create a world that seems to the audience
both believable and exciting.

In every play there are three main elements: characterisation,
action, and dialogue. The characterisation will, of course,
depend on the kind of play which you are writing: if it is a
contemporary drama with a realistic setting, then your
characters should be well-rounded and wholly credible. But a
great deal of children's drama has a strong fantastical element
and therefore the characters may be considerably larger than
life. Take this piece of description from Robert Bolt's *The
Thwarting of Baron Bolligrew*:

> (Jasper, 15th Baron Bolligrew, enters, carring a twelve-bore shotgun.
> He is small but burly, with a red face and black whiskers; choleric
> and selfish but with the fascination of childish greed. He is
> anachronistically dressed in a loud check jacket, bowler hat,
> breeches, gaiters. Accompanying him is Squire Blackheart, huge and
> stupid. He wears black armour, topped by enormous black plumes.
> He moons stolidly throughout the interview, chewing his moustache.)

Clearly these characters will make an impact from the moment
of their first appearance, which is exactly the sort of effect you

need to achieve, especially when writing for younger children. In some kinds of drama, usually those with a strong folk-tale or mythological element, there is even a place for the stereotype, such as the wicked stepmother, the proud princess, the stupid giant – provided, of course, that they can be enlivened by a few original touches.

Stuart Griffiths, in his invaluable book *How Plays are Made*, says that every play has a driver; that is, one character who initiates the action. In *Hamlet*, for example, it is the King; in *Macbeth* it's Lady Macbeth. As you can see, the driver isn't necessarily the main character; on the contrary, he's often the one who creates the problems that the main character has to overcome. A play needs protagonists who are fairly evenly matched in order to create a proper tension; and the audience must be able to sympathize with one of those protagonists, otherwise they won't care about the outcome. The action arises out of conflict and can only be resolved after some sort of change has taken place. Without change there is no drama.

The dialogue should be lively, crisp, and to-the-point. It is best to avoid long speeches when writing for children and to make absolutely sure there are no dull bits. Above all, try to give the actors – whether they are children or professionals – a chance to shine. As a playwright you are very dependent on your actors, and the least you can do for them is to avoid giving them lines to say that are virtually unsayable. Read all your dialogue aloud – and make it a dramatic reading, in the privacy of your room if necessary – before fixing it on paper in your final draft.

The construction of your play is all-important. First you must set the scene and establish your characters as clearly and strongly as possible; then immediately light the fuse that will set the whole drama alight. From that moment on the action should sweep relentlessly forward, building slowly through a number of mini-confrontations until you reach the final stupendous climax. The resolution should be brief and satisfying, so that you send your audience away happy.

121

The layout of a playscript will differ according to the medium for which you are writing, but as it is not possible to give examples of each kind within the scope of this book, I shall suggest sources where you can find the information you need. Generally speaking, however, every script has three components: scene, action, and dialogue. The scene is established first: the action is usually bracketed in order to keep it clearly separated from the dialogue; and the words to be spoken are shown against the name of the speaker.

For example:

Scene: A deserted railway station in the middle of the night. A girl (15) is curled up on a wooden seat, fast asleep. The station-master enters.

STATION-MASTER: Hey-up, what's this? You can't sleep here, Miss. It's against the law.

GIRL: (Waking slowly and rubbing her eyes.) Where am I?

STATION-MASTER: (Indignant) Where are you? You're on my station, that's where you are. And you've missed the last train!

If you observe these general conventions your script will be easy to read and, even if you haven't quite got the details right, may be considered on its merits by anyone looking for a new play.

Plays to be performed by children

Many of the plays written for children today are designed both for reading and for performance. Reading plays aloud is always an enjoyable exercise and some texts work well in a classroom situation: others however, seem flat on the printed page and only spring to life when performed. Anyone who has ever been involved with "the school play" knows how much excitement can be generated by mounting a major production. Fired by "the roar of the greasepaint, the smell of the crowd", children become totally involved with the whole process – acting, costume, make-up, lighting, scene-shifting, even the selling of programmes. It is a corporate activity that offers something to everyone, not just the actors.

Ideally, therefore, your play should be adaptable, so that it can be performed in the round, on a thrust stage, or framed by a proscenium arch. It can be short – twenty-minute one-act dramas are always in demand – or a full three-, four-, or five-act play with or without music. There are no specific limitations as to the number of scenes or the locations where they can be set. These days, having thrown off the shackles of drawing-room drama, audiences will happily accept a scene that's established, with Shakespearean simplicity, by the use of a single prop. Nor need you restrict yourself to a small cast, since the more children who can be given a chance to act the better; and the dialogue should be fairly evenly spread between them. However, this does mean you must take care to make each character memorable, otherwise the audience will become confused. If you want to use incidental music you should give suggestions without being too specific, since the final choice will depend on what the school has available. Schools with a strong musical tradition will welcome a play that allows them to involve their best musicians. Even so, it is advisable to make your score as flexible as possible, so that it can be performed by, say, one piano and a tympanist as well as by a full orchestra.

Subject matter can range from historical realism, such as Bill Owen's *The Ragged School*, which is about the homeless boys rescued by Dr Barnardo, to the crazy comedy of Ken Campbell's *Skungpoomery*. At present there seem to be more plays written for older children to perform than for the primary school age group. Several educational publishers are prepared to consider plays for children, although their needs tend to vary according

123

to the current trends of drama teaching. To find out more I recommend you to read *Plays for Young People to Read and Perform* by Aidan Chambers, a Signal Bookguide obtainable from the The Thimble Press, Lockwood, Station Road, South Woodchester, Stroud, Glos GL5 5EQ.

Puppet plays

There is something strangely hypnotic about a puppet show, and at its best it is undoubtedly an art form in its own right. However, most puppet plays are written – or more accurately extemporised – by the children themselves to feature the puppets they've made in craft lessons. This is in keeping with tradition, since there has always been a strong element of improvisation in puppet plays, from *Punch and Judy* onwards. Nonetheless, there may well be a niche here for the writer who is interested in puppetry, perhaps combining the text with ideas for making the puppets. To find out more about the craft you should contact The Puppet Centre, Battersea Arts Centre, Lavender Hill, London, SW11 5TJ.

Plays for the professional theatre

There are several theatre companies specialising in plays for children, such as the Polka Children's Theatre and the Unicorn Theatre for Children, whose addresses can be found in the *Writers & Artists' Year Book*. The National Theatre also mounts a children's play occasionally. Many of these plays, having received a professional launching, are subsequently performed in schools by child actors, with varying degrees of success. Clearly they make greater demands on both acting skills and production resources than the plays written specifically for children. Nonetheless, some of them are so cleverly crafted and work so superlatively well on stage that they rise triumphantly above any shortcomings in production.

One example is David Wood's musical play *The Plotters of Cabbage Corner*, which was first presented by the Worcester Repertory Company and subsequently mounted at the Shaw Theatre, London. The "plotters" of the title are garden insects threatened by the use of chemical sprays by the Big Ones (human beings). Here David Wood demonstrates how to introduce some audience participation.

> Greenfly enters quickly, hand outstretched as if holding something: she doesn't see Slug but trips over his foot, falling over.
> GREENFLY: (Getting up) Ooh, I was sure I was going to be late, and what happens? I arrive and there's nobody here – maybe they've all overslept. There's no-one here at all!
> (The Audience should shout out that someone is there. Greenfly reacts accordingly – eventually seeing Slug.)
> Ooh! It's Slug – fast asleep – ooh, he's a lazy old thing, he really is. I'd better not wake him up – he can be very nasty sometimes – so I'll wait till the meeting starts.

What every good playwright has – and I suspect it's purely instinctive – is a sense of theatre, the ability to create moments of magic that will stay in the minds of an audience long after the play is over. An extreme example is the spectacular transformation scene in a pantomine, but equally effective can be a single character left on stage, lit only by a spotlight. The moment may be entirely visual, or it may be achieved by words-and-image combined. The writer's task is to create opportunities for this kind of event to take place.

It is probably true to say that most professional playwrights have at one time been actors, or connected with some other aspect of play production. When it comes to knowing what will "work" on stage there is no substitute for experience, so if you are not already involved in some way, I suggest you should join some kind of amateur company, whether adult or juvenile. You may even be able to persuade them to try out your play in performance, so that you can discover where the weak points are, if any, and put them right before sending it off to a publisher.

Radio drama for schools

These days the only real outlet for children's drama on radio is in Schools Broadcasting. To quote from the handbook on *Writing for the BBC*: "The Department is pleased to hear from new writers, who should submit a detailed note of their background or qualifications, a specimen of their written work and a statement of the subject area to which they hope to contribute. You don't need to have high academic qualifications but you should have the ability to research a topic in depth". For further information I suggest you obtain a copy of the handbook from the BBC Shop, 35 Marylebone High Street, London W1M 4AA.

Radio is a wonderfully free and exciting medium for dramatists to explore. Often called the Theatre of the Mind, it imposes no limitations as to sets – you can whisk your actors from Brixton to the Bahamas at no extra expense – and it allows the writer to get right inside his characters in a way that is impossible on television. Your raw materials are (a) voices; (b) sound effects; (c) music; and (d) silence. The voices should, of course, be as varied as possible to avoid confusion on the part of the listener; and sound effects are best used sparingly, to set the scene and create atmosphere. Music can be highly effective in establishing a mood, but background music is distracting and often irritating. Silence is a potent factor, and can be used to regulate the pace of a scene.

When writing for radio there are of course certain conventions that must be observed. William Ash's book *The Way to Write Radio Drama* will help you to understand the complexities of the craft, and to appreciate its potential.

Original TV drama

It would be misleading if I were to give the impression this is an easy field to break into. It is not impossible, but it is very, very difficult for a novice writer to get a play accepted for television. This is partly due to the strong competition – many professional writers earn the bulk of their income from television – and partly to the fact that you need to know something about the medium before you can produce a workable script.

The first advice any television company will give you is to watch their current output. Both the BBC and the independent commercial companies produce some original drama each year, but these productions are costly to mount so they are understandably reluctant to take risks. ITV's *Dramarama* series, in which half-hour plays are produced by various regional companies, can be a good opening for the novice writer.

Technically, of course, you are far more limited when it comes to sets and the number in the cast than when writing for any other medium. On the whole, low-budget plays that make only modest demands on production resources stand the best chance of being considered. These days, however, with increasing use of film and video techniques, requirements are changing all the time; so before embarking on a major project it is a good idea to approach a company with an outline of your idea, together with a few sample pages of the script, to see if they are interested.

If you have a favourite children's novel which you are convinced would make good television, you may like to attempt a dramatisation. First, of course, you have to check that the TV rights are still available by writing to the publisher, who will probably put you in touch with the author's agent. The next step is to prepare a "TV treatment", which takes the form of a story outline and details of studio requirements such as number in the cast, sets, etc. The purpose of this "treatment" is to sell your idea to the television company, so you should make it sound as attractive as possible. And keep it concise – six pages is about the maximum. If a producer is interested, he may invite you to come and talk about it. Then he'll ask you to produce a breakdown of scenes and – if you are thinking in terms of a serial – probably the first half-hour script.

Before you start dramatising a book, it is advisable to read it through at least twice; and on the second reading to pick out the dramatic moments, the "peaks" that carry the story forward. This will give you the shape you need to work on. I must warn you, however, that dramatisation is a highly-skilled business, which is why most television companies prefer to entrust the work to experienced writers.

In fact, writing for television seems like a Catch 22 situation. How can you ever become experienced unless someone will give you that vital first opportunity?

Well, there are ways in which you can improve your chances. For example, several organisations in various parts of the country offer short courses in television drama to the novice writer. Best known, perhaps, are those run by the London Media Workshops. You can obtain details by writing to them at 101 King's Drive, Gravesend, Kent DA12 5BQ. The Arvon Foundation offers courses not only on writing for television and radio but on other aspects of the craft as well, including writing for children: details from The Arvon Foundation at Totleigh Barton, Sheepwash, Devon EX21 5NS. You will also learn a great deal from reading *The Way to Write for Television* by Eric Paice.

If you are really serious about wanting to write for television – and you have to be serious to succeed – then you'd be well advised to study the medium in some depth before you start sending off scripts or treatments to any of the major television companies. If they realise that you have taken time and trouble to learn the craft, they are far more likely to take notice of anything you may submit.

12

MEETING YOUR READERS

This chapter is by way of a postscript, since it deals with one of
the more pleasurable consequences of being a children's writer,
namely that of being invited to speak to groups of children either
in schools or at a local library. I say "pleasurable", because your
audience will almost certainly be honest, lively, and appreciative,
and the feedback you receive on these occasions is invaluable.
However, there are some do's and don'ts which it may be helpful
to mention.

Ideally, the children will have been well prepared for your
visit. Your book has probably been read to them in class and
they may even have done some artwork connected with the
story. They will have seen your name in print and been told that
they are about to meet a real, live author, so the minute you walk
into the room about 30 pairs of eyes will fix themselves on you,
curious to see in what way you differ from ordinary mortals. At
this point you become uncomfortably aware that something
unusual is expected of you and that just being an author isn't
enough: you have to be an entertainer as well.

Your approach will differ, of course, according to the age
group you are addressing. Very young children soon become
restless if you talk *at* them rather than *with* them, and they aren't
likely to be held spellbound by someone nattering on about the
techniques of writing. Some kind of visual aid is essential,
perhaps large-scale drawings of your characters or scenes from
the story. This is where the author/illustrator has such an

advantage. Shirley Hughes says that children seem to relax immediately when she begins to draw, although it does involve enormous concentration to draw *and* hold an audience at the same time.

She recalls with great affection the time when she used to go on tour with the late Dorothy Edwards: "I feel I picked up everything I know about addressing a child audience by being there with Dorothy, drawing pictures while she talked. She had the most natural address to children I've ever encountered – funny, immediate, never patronising to the slightest degree, but always grown-up, by which I mean never trying to 'come down' to their level, which some children's authors try to do with disastrous and embarrassing results. She had, of course, enormously clear and lively recall of her own childhood and a marvellous memory for things other people had told her about theirs. Her love – and respect – for her child audience was always there."

Shirley Hughes also emphasises how important it is for children to be able to talk back to the speaker, so that it becomes more of a conversation than a lecture. This can of course be a problem if you find yourself in a large hall with over 50 children, which means that it may be impossible to hear what those at the back are trying to say – and that you are having to shout in order to make yourself audible. If, during your preliminary discussions with the school, you can suggest that numbers should be limited to about 30, this will undoubtedly make things easier. However, it isn't always possible to do this without disappointing some of the children, in which case you have to manage as best you can.

When speaking to children of about 8-11 you will find it works best if you talk about one particular story you've written rather than about writing in general. If you start by reading short extracts, so that they get the flavour of the book, and then tell them how the idea first came to you and how you developed it, you'll probably be amazed at the range and astuteness of the questions you are asked.

With this age group I generally conclude with a story-building session, in which I ask children to think up a couple of characters, starting in each case with the name, and then to put those characters into a situation. Gradually this begins to build into a story and soon the children are brimming over with suggestions about what happens next. At this stage it takes all my skill as a storyteller to maintain some kind of shape and cohesion, and I have to be prepared for some highly unusual twists and turns of the plot. As soon as we reach a promising cliffhanger, I say, "Right, now it's over to you. You go away and finish it off." Some children will do exactly what you tell them; some will painstakingly reproduce everything you've said, finishing it off with one short sentence; and some will write an entirely different story. None of this matters. The aim is not only to provide a starting point, but also to ensure that your visit may bear some fruit and not merely have been an enjoyable diversion.

Talking to older children requires a different technique again. Some kind of description of your work – not too lengthy – will be necessary at the beginning, partly to break the ice and partly to clear up any misconceptions they may have about writers in general. After that it helps if you can get a dialogue going, which means that you must fairly swiftly establish some kind of rapport with your audience. Adolescents are often reluctant to speak out in front of their peers for fear of sounding foolish, so somehow you have to let them know that you don't mind how obvious or elementary their questions may be – you are prepared to answer anything. Once you've created the right kind of atmosphere you'll be surprised how genuinely interested they are in the whole business of writing. The chances are that some have literary aspirations themselves and are therefore genuinely anxious to know how best to start on a writing career.

There are of course certain hazards lying in wait for the unwary speaker, such as the child who has a nose-bleed in the middle of your talk which totally disrupts everyone's concentration; or the visual aids you've pinned on the wall behind you suddenly descending on your head while you are in mid-flow. On the whole, disciplinary problems don't occur, since there is always a teacher present to frown menacingly at persistent offenders or even, in extreme cases, to eject them from the hall. I remember one particular occasion, however, when I was invited to speak to a group of 7-9 year olds. My talk went well, but afterwards the Head asked if I'd mind speaking again to a class of infants who'd been *so* disappointed not to hear me. What else could I say but yes? She then showed me into a room full of saucer-eyed five-year-olds and LEFT ME TO IT! Totally unprepared, I did the only thing possible and told them a story, while at the same time wiping a few noses and breaking up the odd fight that threatened to break out. Twenty-five minutes later I was relieved – in more ways than one – by the class teacher, by which time I had a strong suspicion that I'd been coerced into baby-sitting while the staff took a tea-break. In all fairness I must say this has only happened to me once: usually the organisation is excellent and the staff very mindful of a writer's comfort and sensibilities.

Do children really get anything out of these visits? You can only hope they receive some sort of stimulation, or at the very least realise that books are written by ordinary, accessible people and not by remote beings living in ivory towers.

For the writer, of course, the rewards are considerable – and I don't mean the financial ones, although these days most schools are able to pay speakers a respectable fee, thanks to funding from regional Arts Councils. But here is a unique opportunity to find out from your readers what they like about your books and what they don't like. Be prepared for total honesty, especially from the very young. And don't just pay attention to the extrovert, the bright, the articulate children, even though they may be the ones you notice most in a group. Look out for the ones who listen raptly but keep quiet when you ask for questions and hang back at the end when the others push forward, clamouring for you to sign your name on scrappy bits of paper. It is these children I often feel drawn to most, because the chances are that they're the *bookish* ones; and therefore they remind me of myself at that age.

And at the end of a visit, if a small girl with serious eyes tugs at my sleeve and whispers, "I liked your book . . . I've read it twice" – well, that's when you know it's all been worth while.

READING LIST

General

Richard Adams: Watership Down (Allen Lane/Kestrel)

Beverley Cleary: *Ramona the Pest* (Hamish Hamilton/Puffin)

Richmal Crompton: *Just William* (Macmillan)

Dianne Doubtfire: *The Craft of Novel-Writing* (Allison & Busby)

Dorothy Edwards: *My Naughty Little Sister* (Methuen/Magnet)

Fiona French: *Snow White in New York* (OUP)

Jane Gardam: *Bridget and William* (Julia MacRae/Puffin)

Kenneth Grahame: *The Wind in the Willows* (Methuen)

Terry Jones: *The Saga of Erik the Viking* (Pavilion)

C. Day Lewis: *The Otterbury Incident* (Bodley Head/Puffin)

Philippa Pearce: *The Way to Sattin Shore* (Kestrel)

Arthur Ransome: *Swallows and Amazons* (Cape/Puffin)

Anna Sewell: *Black Beauty* (Purnell/Puffin)

Mary Treadgold: *We Couldn't Leave Dinah* (Cape/Puffin)

E.B. White: *Charlotte's Web* (Hamish Hamilton/Puffin)

Henry Williamson: *Tarka the Otter* (Webb & Bower/Puffin)

Diana Wynne Jones: *The Time of the Ghost* (Macmillan/Beaver)

The Signal Approach to Children's Fiction (Kestrel/The Thimble Press)

Writers, Critics and Children, ed. Geoffrey Fox, Graham Hammond, Terry Jones, Frederic Smith and Keneth Sterck (Heinemann)

Under-sevens

Janet and Allan Ahlberg: *The Jolly Postman* (Heinemann)

Val Biro: *Gumdrop: The Adventures of a Vintage Car* (Hodder & Stoughton)

John Burningham: *Mr Gumpy's Outing* (Jonathan Cape)

Dorothy Butler: *Babies Need Books* (Bodley Head)

Eric Carle: *The Very Hungry Caterpillar* (Hamish Hamilton)

Babette Cole: *Princess Smartypants* (Hamish Hamilton)

Shirley Hughes: *Moving Molly* (Bodley Head/Fontana Lions)

Shirley Hughes: *Dogger* (Bodley Head/Fontana Lions)

Shirley Hughes: *An Evening at Alfie's* (Bodley Head)

Pat Hutchins: *Rosie's Walk* (Bodley Head/Puffin)

Leo Leonni: *Little Blue and Little Yellow* (Hodder & Stoughton)

Jan Pienkowski: *The Haunted House Pop-up Book* (Heinemann)

Elfrida Vipont: *The Elephant and the Bad Baby* (Hamish Hamilton)

Thomas & Wanda Zacharias: *But Where is the Green Parrot?* (Chatto & Windus)

Young Adults

Lynn Reid Banks: *My Darling Villain* (Bodley Head)

Anthea Cohen: *Substance and Shadow* (Severn House/Pan)

Robert Cormier: *I am the Cheese* (Gollancz)

Anita Desai: *The Village by the Sea* (Heinemann/Puffin)

Farrukh Dhondy: *Come to Mecca* (Collins/Fontana Lions)

Paula Fox: *The Moonlight Man* (Dent)

Jane Gardam: *A Long Way from Verona* (Hamish Hamilton/Abacus)

Alan Garner: *The Owl Service* (Collins/Fontana Lions)

William Golding: *The Lord of the Flies* (Faber)

Janni Howker: *The Nature of the Beast* (Julia MacRae)

M.E. Kerr: *Dinky Hocker Shoots Smack!* (Gollancz)

E.L. Konigsburg: *Journey by First Class Camel* (Hamish Hamilton)

Mary Melford: *The Watcher Bee* (André Deutsch)

K.M. Peyton: *Flambards* (OUP/Puffin)

J.D. Salinger: *The Catcher in the Rye* (Coles Pub. Co/Penguin)

Jill Paton Walsh: *Unleaving* (Macmillan)

Paul Zindel: *The Pigman* (Bodley Head/Puffin)

Fantasy and science fiction

Joan Aiken: *The Wolves of Willoughby Chase* (Cape/Puffin)

Lucy M. Boston: *The Children of Green Knowe* (Faber/Puffin)

John Christopher: *The Guardians* (Hamish Hamilton/Puffin)

Susan Cooper: *The Dark is Rising* (Chatto & Windus/Puffin)

Roald Dahl: *James and the Giant Peach* (Allen & Unwin/ Puffin)

Penelope Farmer: *Charlotte Sometimes* (Chatto & Windus/ Puffin)

Alan Garner: *Elidor* (Collins/Puffin)

Robert A. Heinlein: *Between Planets* (Gollancz)

Tove Jansson: *Finn Family Moomintroll* (Puffin)

Clive King: *Stig of the Dump* (Hamish Hamilton/Puffin)

C.S. Lewis: *The Lion, the Witch and the Wardrobe* (Collins/ Fontana Lions)

Penelope Lively: *Astercote* (Heinemann/Piccolo)

Jan Mark: *Divide and Rule* (Kestrel)

John Masefield: *The Box of Delights* (Heinemann/Puffin)

E. Nesbitt: *Five Children and It* (Puffin)

J.R.R. Tolkien: *The Hobbit* (Allen & Unwin)

P.L. Travers: *Mary Poppins* (Collins/Puffin)

Non-fiction

Gwynneth Ashby: *Korean Village* (A & C Black)

Laurene Krasny Brown and Marc Brown: *Visiting an Exhibition* (Collins)

Moira Butterfield: *Air Travel Games* (Usborne)

Adrian Davies: *Discovering Squirrels* (Wayland)

Margery Fisher: *Matters of Fact* (Brockhampton Press)

Ann Hoffman: *Research for Writers* (A & C Black)

Robin Kerrod: *Sound and Vision* (Grafton Books)

Microfun Puzzles (Franklin Watts)

Brian Ward: *Diet and Nutrition* (Franklin Watts)

Drama

William Ash: *The Way to Write Radio Drama* (Elm Tree Books)

Robert Bolt: *The Thwarting of Baron Bolligrew* (Heinemann/ Samuel French)

Ken Campbell: *Skungpoomery* (Methuen)

Aidan Chambers: *Plays for Young People to Read and Perform* (Signal: The Thimble Press)

Stuart Griffiths: *How Plays are Made* (Heinemann Educational Books)

Bill Owen: *The Ragged School* (Macmillan Education)

Eric Paice: *The Way to Write for Television* (Elm Tree Books)

Ian Watson: *Conversations with Ayckbourn* (Macdonald Futura)

David Wood: *The Plotters of Cabbage Patch Corner* (Samuel French)

INDEX

INDEX

INDEX